Diplomatic Wives

Published to coincide with its première, *Diplomatic Wives* opened at the Palace Theatre, Watford, in March 1989.

Louise Page was born in London in 1955 and brought up in Sheffield. She read Drama and Theatre Arts at Birmingham University and, in 1979, she became Yorkshire Television's Fellow in Drama and Television at the University of Sheffield. Her stage plays include *Want-Ad* (Birmingham Arts Lab, 1977; ICA, 1979); *Lucy* (Bristol New Vic Studio, 1979); *Tissue* (Birmingham Repertory Theatre, 1978; ICA, 1978; adapted for Radio 4, 1979); *Hearing* (Birmingham Repertory Theatre, 1979); *Flaws* (Sheffield University Drama Studio, 1980): *Housewives* (Derby Playhouse, 1981 a Radio/Theatre production); *Salonika* (Royal Court Theatre Upstairs, 1982; winner of the George Devine Award); *Real Estate* (Tricycle Theatre, London, 1984) and *Golden Girls* (Royal Shakespeare Company, The Other Place, Stratford-upon-Avon, 1984) *Beauty and the Beast* (jointly commissioned by the The Women's Playhouse Trust and Methuen) opened at the Liverpool Playhouse in November 1985 before transferring to the Old Vic, London in December 1985. She was awarded the first J T Grein Award for Drama by the Critic's Circle. She has also written for radio and television.

by the same author

BEAUTY AND THE BEAST

GOLDEN GIRLS

REAL ESTATE

SALONIKA

PLAYS BY WOMEN: VOLUME ONE
(*Vinegar Tom*, Caryl Churchill; *Dusa, Fish, Stas, and Vi*, Pam Gems; *Tissue*, Louise Page; *Aurora Leigh* adapted by Micheline Wandor from Elizabeth Barret Browning's verse novel.)

Louise Page

Diplomatic Wives

METHUEN DRAMA

A METHUEN MODERN PLAY
First published in Great Britain in 1989 by Methuen Drama,
Michelin House, 81 Fulham Road, London SE3 6RB and
distributed in the United States of America by HEB Inc.,
70 Court Street, Portsmouth, New Hampshire 03801.

British Library Cataloguing in Publication Data

Page, Louise, *1955* —
    Diplomatic wives.— (Methuen modern plays)
    I. Title
    822'.914

    ISBN 0-413-61430-1

Printed by Expression Printers,
39 North Road, London N7 9DP.

CAUTION
All rights whatsoever in this play are strictly reserved and
applications for permission to perform it in whole or in part must
be made in advance, before rehearsals begin, to Goodwin
Associates, 12 Rabbit Row, Kensington Church Street, London
W8 4DX.

To Lou, from Louise.
Thank You.

Diplomatic Wives was first performed at the Palace Theatre, Watford on 2 March 1989, with the following cast:

CHRIS MELBOURNE	Charlotte Cornwell
JOHN MELBOURNE	Will Knightly
LIBBY WEBSTER	Anna Carteret

Directed by   Lou Stein
Designed by   Martin Sutherland
Lighting by   Rory Dempster

ACT ONE

Scene One

Darkness.

Very loud the sound of a plane taking off.

In light we see CHRIS *waving some sort of garment. Huge waving in the hope of it being visible to a passenger on the plane.*

CHRIS. 'Bye! 'Bye! See you in England. We'll miss you.

She waves again.

Suddenly she becomes aware of what she is waving with – it's a sort of baseball jacket that obviously belongs to her stepson, KIT . *She looks at it.*

Oh Kit, you fool! I warned you.

I'll miss you.

Her eyes follow the disappearing plane.

She looks round the airport, she is looking for her husband JOHN *who is late.*

She looks at her watch.

She looks in her purse to see if she has money for the phone.

She feels in the pocket of the jacket.

In the pocket there are a couple of cassettes.

She looks at them and puts them back.

She looks round for JOHN.

Her attention turns to the jacket.

She smooths the jacket and folds it up.

She tries to put it in her handbag but it won't fit.

She looks at her watch again.

She's getting very frustrated.

She makes a move as if she is going to make a decision, ie, in the direction of a desk to ask if a message has been left for her.

She doesn't complete the move, she stops and hesitates.

She says to herself.

Christine!

She tries again to get the jacket in her handbag.

She gets the jacket in the bag by taking a book out of it. But the jacket distorts the bag dreadfully, its elegance is all gone.

She glances round the airport again.

Then having no other option she sits down and opens the book.

She sees somebody she thinks might be JOHN .

She stands up.

It's not, she sits down to read again.

There is an announcement in Arabic about the plane from Nairobi being late. CHRIS *obviously understands the message because she looks at her watch again and then returns to the book.*

At the moment the book becomes her focus of attention JOHN *enters. He carries a briefcase.* CHRIS *puts her book down, open.*

Kit said you'd bring your briefcase!

JOHN. Darling, I'm sorry.

He picks up the book and closes it.

You'll break the spine.

He glances into the front of the book.

American Embassy?

CHRIS. It's not in ours.

JOHN (*handing the book to her*). Good, you can fill me in on Dr Webster.

CHRIS (*reading the jacket*). 'Dr Webster lives on a smallholding near Harlech with her husband. She has no children.'

JOHN. She knows her subject. Did I take you to Harlech to measure the dungeons?

CHRIS. Someone else. You've lost my place!

JOHN. The spine's broken. It'll fall open.

CHRIS. It's a paperback. How else does one read it? I couldn't read it. I couldn't concentrate.

JOHN. The demography of population expansion's hardly airport reading!

CHRIS. John, Kit's plane took off an hour late and you weren't here! We were worried.

JOHN. Any news on the Nairobi flight?

CHRIS. It's rescheduled for half past.

JOHN. Does nothing in this country get anywhere on time?

CHRIS. Not even her Britannic Majesty's First Secretary.

JOHN. Missed Kit, early for Dr Webster. So much for killing two birds with one stone!

CHRIS. Kit could have gone on a plane which got him to London at a decent time and you could have come back for Dr Webster.

JOHN. Flying children out for half term's not official.

CHRIS. Then why did you do it?

JOHN. He's my son. I wanted to see him. I love him.

CHRIS. That isn't how it looks.

JOHN. Darling, we were sorting out the Queen's Birthday Party!

CHRIS. You were supposed to be sorting out your son going back to school!

JOHN. Darling, we still don't have a definite on the asparagus.

CHRIS. Damn, your asparagus!

JOHN. Darling, you suggested it.

CHRIS. Not as the be all and end all! Have strawberries! No they grow strawberries here! Have raspberries!

JOHN. We have got lumbered with Tunisia's QBP as well.

CHRIS. So I got lumbered with Kit?

JOHN. Darling, I simply couldn't –

CHRIS. Oh, darling –

Her mood changes.

Jagger's being kicked out in disgrace is hardly reason for them to dump their QBP on us.

JOHN. There's no Second Secretary at the moment either. And it's more than just the QBP. The Tunisians have got to know we're not apologising for Jagger.

CHRIS. Why don't we just send someone over to replace him?

JOHN. Then who'd deal with the flight path negotiations?

CHRIS. Not to mention the violet root rot in the Evesham asparagus crop! Why do you assume it would have to be you?

JOHN. Who else is there? It's sensitive. It's got to be absolutely the right person and they've got to have Arabic and French.

CHRIS. We're all got Arabic and French. Was there no one this afternoon, even for a couple of hours?

JOHN. Christine, I knew I could rely on you.

CHRIS. And you love your son!

JOHN. Would I have left him with you if I didn't? My two favourite people?

CHRIS. Are we?

JOHN. Was Kit being a pain?

CHRIS. Kit's not a pain.

JOHN. You –

CHRIS. I know. I suppose I got to know him this holiday.

JOHN. You were a brick.

CHRIS. He insisted on buying the second round of refreshments. It was terribly sweet. And terribly like you.

JOHN. He can't have been minding that much. Anyway, he's used to it.

CHRIS. That's what he said.

JOHN. Yes, but what did he mean?

CHRIS. That he was used to you not being there when you said you would be, I suppose.

JOHN. And you agreed?

CHRIS. I'm telling you what Kit said. He has hardly seen you all week.

JOHN. I didn't see my father for months at a time.

CHRIS. Did you never resent it?

JOHN. It's the way Kit's life's always been. He understands.

CHRIS. Does he?

JOHN. I once got hauled over the coals by my boss because I couldn't get a babysitter for my son. She called me unprofessional.

But she won't rise.

CHRIS. You had promised him. 'Whatever happens' you said at breakfast.

JOHN. And I meant it.

CHRIS. You didn't mean it because you didn't keep it.

JOHN. That's unfair. But once I thought I'd missed him, what was the point?

CHRIS. The point is, he doesn't want to come again.

JOHN. Of course he does.

CHRIS. Not the Whitsun half term. He'd rather stay in England and play cricket.

JOHN. We played cricket!

CHRIS. You, me and Kit. A bat and stump and a ball! We're not exactly a team!

JOHN. If he can't spend a week –

CHRIS. It's where his friends are.

JOHN. He never said this to me.

CHRIS. Perhaps if you'd spent more time with him.

JOHN. I knew I was missing him.

CHRIS. Then don't send him away.

JOHN. He has to be educated. Of course, if Kit's not happy –

CHRIS. He must be happy if he wants to stay there for half term – or it doesn't say much about his home life. I gave him 20 pounds from you.

JOHN. Twenty? Twenty, doesn't go far at home any more, does it?

CHRIS. That was all the sterling I had.

JOHN *takes out his wallet.*

That's not what I meant.

JOHN *carefully takes out 20 pounds and gives it to Chris.*

I shouldn't have to explain your broken promises to your son.

She takes the money from JOHN

Thank you.

JOHN. Remind me to ring him.

Pause.

Will you?

CHRIS. I wasn't the one arranging the QBP.

JOHN. I'll explain to him. Just don't let me forget.

CHRIS. Again.

JOHN. I didn't forget.

CHRIS. He never crossed your mind!

JOHN. He did actually Christine. He did.

CHRIS. Did we?

JOHN. I'll ring him when he gets to London. Does that make you feel better?

CHRIS. It's not my conscience he should be on.

JOHN. He's not on my conscience.

CHRIS *is exultant.*

Of course he's on my conscience but that's not why I'm ringing him.

CHRIS. He was worried about you.

JOHN. Why?

CHRIS. Because we thought you would be here.

JOHN. Okay. I'm sorry you had to deal with it. But you did say you weren't doing anything.

CHRIS. Only Dr Webster's visit and dinner for 14 –

JOHN. Yes, but nothing –

CHRIS. No, nothing at important as the Queen's Birthday Party. How riveting that would have been for your captors!

JOHN. Kit's not been going through all that again?

CHRIS. You weren't here when you said you would be!

JOHN. Just because Bloggs minor or whoever's father –

CHRIS. Would you want a son who didn't care?

JOHN. Darling, kidnaps happen to other people.

CHRIS. Not when Kit and I are sitting waiting for you.

JOHN. I don't know where Kit gets his imagination from.

CHRIS. You were late. Of course he was worried.

JOHN. Worry about me when we're in Europe. It's when people feel safe that –

CHRIS. What?

JOHN. I'm not in that league.

CHRIS. We love you John. We can't not worry. He wanted to know what would happen –

JOHN. Nothing's going to happen.

CHRIS. He thinks – he wanted to know if he'd be left with Vee?

JOHN. Since she's practically the only family of any description that he's got – Who does he want as his legal guardian?

He looks at CHRIS

You didn't want the responsibility. You were adamant.

Vee's my sister. She'd hardly exclude you.

Pause.

CHRIS. Wouldn't you want me to have him?

JOHN. I didn't –

CHRIS. Why not?

JOHN. If something happened to me wouldn't you want to go back to the Foreign Office?

CHRIS. Kit would be a bit of you!

JOHN. Are you asking me?

CHRIS. I could have been his mother just now.

JOHN. It wasn't something you wanted.

CHRIS. I didn't understand then. It's the everyday that's the real responsibility. The fetching and carrying. I couldn't bear losing Kit as well.

JOHN. Christine, you're not to ransom, you're never to deal. Promise.

Pause.

Chris, you'd be throwing it all away.

CHRIS. Because I loved you?

JOHN. Once there'd been one deal there could be another. I'd be too vunerable.

CHRIS. Another promising career bites the dust!

JOHN. Christine, you had a choice.

CHRIS. No, I thought I had a choice. Every day I lose touch. Every decision that you make. Every secret that you keep. Every dinner party when I am not supposed to hear the conversation.

JOHN. Are you asking me?

CHRIS. You know I'm not. But I know there are things.

JOHN. Darling, if there was anything you needed to know.

CHRIS. I'd condemn you if you broke official confidences for me.

JOHN. A true professional. Henry was saying that this afternoon.

CHRIS. About me? Why?

JOHN. All hands on deck for the QBP I suppose.

CHRIS. Oh, domestic! Once I used to change my route to work every morning. Now I sit in Cairo's filthy traffic jams with my windows wound down.

JOHN. That's plain silly.

CHRIS. What do I know that's still relevant? My knowlege is five years out of date. I'm not worth anything to anybody.

JOHN. You are to me.

CHRIS. What?

JOHN. Well – you're my wife.

CHRIS. Your bloody wife!

JOHN. Would you like me to get you a coffee?

CHRIS. You sound just like Kit. I've been drinking coffee for hours.

Pause.

Sorry, I didn't say that to rub it in.

She notices a paper cup on the floor.

She picks it up and scrunches it.

There's nothing you can't tell me about life as a paper cup. You do the important thing which is the containing and when you're not containing you're disposable.

She puts the scrunched up cup into her bag.

Kit forgot his jacket and I warned him!

She picks up the book and flicks at it.

JOHN. It's not too late for a child.

CHRIS. If it was mine I could never send it away.

JOHN. Fill me in on Dr Webster's ideas.

CHRIS. Fill yourself in!

She throws the book at him.

The pages go everywhere.

JOHN *is embarrassed.*

CHRIS *makes no move to collect them.*

I can't even read for myself!

JOHN. Do you want to take a taxi home and I'll meet Dr Webster?

CHRIS. I'm here now, aren't I? Your wife is by your side.

JOHN. She's had a rough ride in Kenya.

CHRIS *says nothing.*

Not the sort of thing you expect from them.

CHRIS *doesn't even look at him.*

They didn't let her speak.

Silence.

She was booed off the platform. Apparently she'd hardly opened her mouth.

He hands her back the collected up book.

That's all I know from the telex.

CHRIS *takes the book from him.*

She begins to put the pages in order.

JOHN *opens his briefcase and gets a copy of* LIBBY WEBSTER's *CV*

JOHN. The good doctor's details.

CHRIS. I've seen them. I picked them up from the embassy. Professional habits die hard. How did you think I knew the title of her book?

JOHN. She was up at Bristol when we were there.

CHRIS. I've been trying but I can't place her. I didn't have much truck with the medical fac.

JOHN. We had a scrum-half called Webster –

CHRIS. How do you expect to be properly briefed about her when the Embassy hasn't even got a copy of her book in the library?

JOHN. We'll have to get Erica another copy.

CHRIS. Perhaps Dr Webster will be like the liver transplant expert and present us with a signed copy!

JOHN. Perhaps Dr Webster won't be so vain.

We hear the sound of a plane coming in to land.

JOHN *looks at his watch.*

JOHN. My God. Darling, she's had a rough ride. Try and smile.

CHRIS *smiles a sickly smile.*

Naturally.

CHRIS. If it was natural, I'd be smiling. Why is it that women's smiling is supposed to change everything?

JOHN (*bustling things into his briefcase*). Just try and look happy then. Who are you sitting her next to?

CHRIS. Erica.

JOHN *shuts his briefcase. It is deliberate.*

The woman that wrote this book –

JOHN. Who wrote this –

CHRIS. The woman who wrote this book deserves better than sitting next to Henry and being asked how she got all those brains in her pretty little head. Particularly if she's just had a rough ride.

JOHN. That sort of woman's not pretty.

CHRIS. That won't stop him saying it!

JOHN. He doesn't mean anything by it, you know that.

CHRIS. That's the sting.

JOHN. Sit her next to me.

CHRIS. You haven't read her book! What are you going to talk to her about?

JOHN. We'll have Bristol in common.

CHRIS. You can boast again about being the only student who never went on a demonstration!

JOHN. She can't sit next to Erica. I'll never hear the end of it.

CHRIS. If I sit her next to Henry, Libby Webster will never hear the end of it!

JOHN. You aren't a stupid woman!

CHRIS. Life would be easier.

JOHN. Why do you put yourself down?

CHRIS. You won't even accept the way I set a table!

JOHN. You know the niceness of things is important.

CHRIS. Niceness – This isn't the place to argue, but for once we have fifteen minutes on our own in a place where we are strangers.

JOHN. You know how quickly they disembark them here.

CHRIS (*ice*). If Libby Webster's bored rigid I hope she'll understand it's all for the good of your career. And I hope, when you get Moscow or Washington, she'll consider the sacrifice worthwhile.

JOHN (*to lighten it*). Or Paris.

CHRIS. With your French, you must be joking!

She realises it's cheap.

I used to know how to use an argument to persuade.

JOHN. Christine, you know that as far as I'm concerned you can sit anyone next to anyone but it's –

CHRIS. Do you know the hours of my life I've wasted trying to make sure I got the placements right? I used to sit in Geneva in a flat spin, with my secretary ringing round trying to find me an escort and enough bright, preferably pretty women who weren't on diets to balance the numbers. I couldn't believe my luck when I heard I was getting a widower as my number two.

Pause.

I truly believed you'd be enough. That loving would be

enough. That you needed me enough. I could see when I looked in a mirror that you'd touched me. What do you want?

JOHN. Christine, if you could tell me I'd give it you.

JOHN reaches out to CHRIS .

It's the colour of your dress. It doesn't suit you. It makes you look washed out.

CHRIS. You bought it me!

JOHN. When we were in Europe. The light is different here. Colours change.

He wants to offer her some consolation.

But she is, and she stays for a moment, just out of his reach.

CHRIS. I'll change when we get home.

She looks in the direction of where the disembarking passengers arrive.

CHRIS. They're coming off.

JOHN. Will you ask Yusef to bring the car to the front?

She nods.

She now tries to get the book in her bag.

It's a problem.

JOHN stands with his hand out to take it.

Suddenly she is aware of this.

She hands it to him.

She smiles, glad to have the problem solved.

She looks in the direction of where people are arriving.

CHRIS. Your Dr Webster is probably that frumpy one.

She goes off in the direction that JOHN came from.

JOHN walks towards the arrivals holding the book high so LIBBY WEBSTER can see it and know it's her he's come to meet.

He stands looking for a moment.

LIBBY WEBSTER *enters.*

She is attractive, but you know clothes aren't a concern.

LIBBY. I think you're looking for me?

JOHN. You!

LIBBY. I hope so.

JOHN. Libby Webster?

LIBBY. Yes.

JOHN. This Libby Webster?

LIBBY. John, it's not a book you see people reading by chance!

JOHN. Really, I'm finding it very interesting and most readable.

LIBBY. You're still doing your preparation at the last minute!

JOHN. You always could see straight through me.

LIBBY. On that.

JOHN. Anything I say will be a cliché.

LIBBY. Probably. Has it ever stopped you before?

They both talk together.

BOTH. I'll go first!

They laugh.

BOTH. You haven't changed at all.

More laughter.

BOTH. Liar.

LIBBY. John, stop.

JOHN. Liz, shut up.

They laugh and then they pause.

LIBBY. May I? I had the advantage. I knew from the itinerary.

She holds out her hand to shake his.

JOHN. We'd seen Bristol on your CV.

LIBBY. It's my marriage making a chameleon of me. I can travel
through the world as someone completely other.

JOHN. Was he the scrum-half?

LIBBY. Pardon.

JOHN. There was a Webster who played rugger.

LIBBY. John, can we shake hands?

JOHN shakes hands with her. She holds on to his hand – perhaps holding it in both hers.

LIBBY. George is a dentist, a retired dentist. It's older men now.

JOHN. Are they more reliable?

LIBBY. About some things.

They break the handshake.

I'm sorry he's not your friend.

JOHN. Webster wasn't a friend. And second 15 material really.

LIBBY. It's so good to see you John, Nairobi wasn't nice.

JOHN. I've heard. Just a telex, not all the details of course.

LIBBY. You will! The look on your face was so wonderful!

JOHN. You could have passed on a message.

LIBBY. I couldn't resist the surprise.

JOHN. Hardly fair when I'm in the heart attack bracket.

LIBBY. There'd have been a doctor on hand!

JOHN (*just looking at her*). I can't reconcile this, you and my history tutor. I assumed you were a professor somewhere by now.

LIBBY. It's nice to be remembered.

JOHN. How could I forget? What happened to history?

LIBBY. It was long time ago. That's why it's history. You laid great emphasis on its being rewritten. I wanted to do something useful in the world. Contribute. I can't tell you what it was like being a student again. Medicine, a vocation and I take it up at 31. But George was always there saying there weren't any obstacles which made it much easier and now I'm here.

JOHN. You look wonderful. Are you?

LIBBY. I'm glad to be here. And not just because of Kenya. But how are you? I thought you'd be beyond the meeting at airports stage. And how is Tessa and – Christopher? Christopher John Fitzroy Melbourne?

JOHN. Kit.

LIBBY. Thank God. But that was the only information I had on him.

JOHN. He's 13. Fourteen just before Christmas.

LIBBY. Tessa sent me one of those name and weight announcements in a Christmas card.

JOHN. I hadn't realised she kept in touch.

LIBBY. She sent it to the university after I'd resigned. It was forwarded to my parents. I remember it because it was the day I met George. New Year's Eve appropriately enough. Is Tessa here?

Pause.

Fifteen years with George. I assume people are still married to the last person they were married to. I'm still rash. Still front-running with the fools and angels.

JOHN. Liz, Tess is dead. She died seven years ago.

LIBBY. Oh my God.

JOHN. It was a terrible shock.

LIBBY. John, I'm so sorry.

JOHN. It was quick. I was assured there was no pain – but you can't know can you?

LIBBY. People feel pain in different ways.

JOHN. Yes.

LIBBY. It must have hurt you.

She takes his hand.

JOHN. I'd thought it would last.

She squeezes his wedding ring hand.

She looks at the ring.

I married Christine McAvoy.

Then he snaps out of it.

Is that all your luggage?

LIBBY. After leaving Bristol I did a year of VSO. It taught me a lot, not to hang on to baggage that wasn't needed on voyage, I try to travel light.

JOHN *reaches out for her bag.*

JOHN. Let me.

LIBBY. I can manage.

JOHN. Please.

Because he's obviously going to insist she gives it to him.

Christine and the car are at the front.

He picks up the bag and starts to exit.

LIBBY *follows asking questions.*

LIBBY. Do you have a chauffeur?

JOHN. With the traffic in this city it takes hours.

They exit.

We hear a plane taking off.

Scene Two

LIBBY's *room in* CHRIS *and* JOHN's *house. It is a nice room. It contains various things that* CHRIS *and* JOHN *have picked up on their travels.*

LIBBY *is unpacking.*

She takes a lot of badly folded clothes out of her bag and dumps them on the bed. She finds what she is looking for, books and papers. She takes them to the dressing table. She goes back to the case to get something else. She strews the floor with stuff from the case. She sits down at the dressing table and begins to try to work. She looks up and sees herself in the dressing table mirror.

She looks at herself for a moment.

She is looking to see how she's aged.

She looks down at her papers and then she looks in the mirror again.

She gets up and goes to the bathroom returning with a towel that she drapes over the mirror.

She sits down to work.

She peeps under the towel.

CHRIS (*off*). Liz?

LIBBY (*dropping the towel*). Come in.

> CHRIS *enters with drinks. She has changed and looks diplomatically elegant.*

CHRIS. Libby! Sorry.

LIBBY. It's all right. I still answer.

CHRIS. You must prefer it. You use it on your books.

LIBBY. Libby's George's name for me.

CHRIS. It never crossed my mind.

LIBBY. Why should you remember me? Christine Melbourne, I wouldn't have thought anything of.

CHRIS. No! Why didn't you let us know? Nairobi would have passed on a message.

LIBBY. I don't know.

She takes the drink.

Safe ice?

CHRIS. Special recipe. You boil the water for three minutes.

LIBBY. I know it seems a fuss.

CHRIS. No, you have work to do. We still worry about water and ice and we've been here two years.

LIBBY. Cheers. I need this.

CHRIS. Welcome.

She can't resist picking something off the floor.

LIBBY. I was just trying to find some papers!

CHRIS. I could send you someone to help unpack.

LIBBY. No. I mean it's only a few bits and pieces.

She grabs the garment off CHRIS.

CHRIS. If there's anything you want pressed.

LIBBY. I've found this wonderful stuff which doesn't crease. You stand up and they all just drop out.

CHRIS. You will make yourself feel at home.

LIBBY. You're very kind.

CHRIS. We're saving the government money, not putting you in a hotel.

LIBBY. I hope they spend it wisely.

CHRIS. Asparagus and new potatoes.

LIBBY. Pardon.

CHRIS. Next Thursday's the event of the year. The Queen's Birthday Party. We entertain in as English a style as possible. Asparagus from Evesham. New potatoes from Jersey.

LIBBY. I was buying Egyptian new potatoes before I left!

CHRIS. Yes.

LIBBY *shakes her head.*

LIBBY. I'd have insisted on a hotel.

CHRIS. John and I are very pleased to have you. Let me give some of this to Yusef. His ironing's better without steam than mine is with it.

CHRIS *picks up something else. It's fancy underwear.*

LIBBY. It's so if I drop dead on the lecture platform they'll know it's clean. And I know I've got it on.

She grabs it off CHRIS.

I know it's ridiculous.

CHRIS. Sometimes one needs all the help one can get.

LIBBY. You don't have to ask anyone.

CHRIS. For me it was perfume. Fortunately the travelling
stopped it being too prohibitive! Did you always?

LIBBY. When I was teaching you and John, yes.

CHRIS. You mean this was underneath all those inspirational
tutorials?

LIBBY. Why not?

CHRIS. You argued with John because he was the only student
who always wore a suit. If he'd known about this. You dark
horse!

LIBBY. Would you trust anyone without a few failings?
Oneself's the hardest person to keep in line. People who can
be that strict with themselves. Think what they could be with
other people?

CHRIS. I can bring you other pillows if you prefer not to have
feathers.

LIBBY. Feathers are fine.

And she desparately needs reassurance.

Was I inspirational?

CHRIS. Yes. You changed the way I saw the world. I stopped
being grateful.

LIBBY. What for?

CHRIS. All the things I'd been brought up to be grateful for.
My education. My family. My luck. That it was all to do with
other people as much as myself. I'm sorry, personally sorry
about Nairobi.

LIBBY. Thank you. Did they tell you?

CHRIS. Not why.

LIBBY. I was doing my best.

CHRIS. We all know that.

LIBBY. No doubt you'll hear.

CHRIS. Sooner or later. Diplomacy's about secrets. There's
always a lot of gossip.

LIBBY *looks at her.*

If you've got a copy of your lecture, I'd like to read it.

LIBBY goes to a table and sorts some papers.

LIBBY. That is what I was going to say.

She reads through the start of it.

If you wouldn't mind I'd prefer John not to read it.

CHRIS. No, of course not.

But LIBBY *hesitates.*

I would like to. Even if you gave it to John personally he'd never find the time.

LIBBY. He thought I'd believe he'd read my book.

CHRIS. I'm sure he would have done so if he'd known it was by you.

LIBBY hands her the papers.

Thank you. It won't go beyond me.

LIBBY. I'd like to know honestly what you think. It was so hard to write. Hard anyway and George was determined to interrupt. We agree every week, I have a certain number of working days and the others are, George calls them sharing – it was the first day it was really nice enough to work outside. He was determined to put up a fence to keep the foxes from the chickens. He dropped the fence post relentlessly until I gave in and held it up for him.

CHRIS. Why Harlech?

LIBBY. It's a nice place. George wanted somewhere he could have animals.

CHRIS. Kit always wants us to have pets. How can we!

LIBBY. The animals take up George's time. He says he talks to them when I'm away.

CHRIS. I can't promise I'll have time to read this until we've got through the QBP. You are expected to put in an appearance by the way. And even if you don't, you won't have any privacy, people do tend to swarm.

She goes to the dressing table drawer to check it's got a key.

She locks it and unlocks it.

We lock anything that's got a key.

About the key.

It fits all the drawers.

She marks the towel and the mirror.

Would you like another towel?

LIBBY. I didn't want to look up and see myself.

CHRIS. Why don't I move you. The view's not as good but you'd have a desk.

LIBBY. Christine, stop trying.

CHRIS *pauses*.

Even at Bristol you tried so hard.

CHRIS. There seemed to be rules. Everybody else seemed to know them

LIBBY. Did I know them?

CHRIS. You seemed to.

LIBBY. I should have supported you against Fraser.

CHRIS. I realised why you couldn't.

LIBBY. I always felt that I owed you an apology for that. That I should have written.

CHRIS. John and Tessa wrote.

LIBBY. Yes.

CHRIS. Tess always was good at that, keeping people informed. And anyway when I came back from Oman I didn't want to go back to Bristol and do a history MA. I wanted to be a diplomat and represent the best country in the world.

LIBBY. Do you still think it's the best?

CHRIS (*avoiding the issue*). There are many worse countries.

LIBBY. But the best?

CHRIS. Libby, please –

LIBBY. You and John always had opinions. That's why you were good to teach. Why I remember you, when I've forgotten others.

CHRIS. I'd hardly represent a country – of course there are things, but it's like your family, you feel disloyal if you say –

LIBBY. You could still stand up for what you believe in.

CHRIS. I'm John's wife. I have to think of him too.

LIBBY. Of his job?

CHRIS. My loyalty's to John.

LIBBY. And what John wants?

CHRIS. John's always known what he wanted. And I've always known too. You knew. You used to argue enough with him about it at Bristol.

LIBBY. You have to admire the nerve of a 20-year-old who announces he's going to be British Ambassador to Washington.

CHRIS. Knowing what he wanted always made him seem so much older than the rest of us.

LIBBY. Yes it did.

CHRIS. Did you recognise him at the airport?

LIBBY. Instantly.

CHRIS. So did I the first day he walked in to work for me. It seemed terribly strange that I was the one doing the explaining and giving the orders. And delegating to John the jobs I didn't want to do.

LIBBY. Don't you miss it?

CHRIS. How could we have had two careers, when there was really nowhere we called home. And I wanted John. And I might not get paid for being his wife but it is part of his job, the entertaining and everything. It's interesting for us to be able to have people like you to stay.

LIBBY. You always were a hostess. I remember the party you gave at Bristol –

CHRIS. Where John got engaged to Tessa?

LIBBY. You didn't even find the time to read Fraser's article.

CHRIS. It would probably have depressed me horribly.

She picks up some things.

Do let me move you. I should have thought that you needed to work.

LIBBY. I'm perfectly happy. All I need is a card table or something.

CHRIS. Card tables we can do you in multiple.

LIBBY. That would be perfect.

CHRIS. My predecessor was a bridge fanatic.

LIBBY. George plays every Wednesday.

CHRIS. I suppose it was one way of passing the time.

LIBBY. I suppose it was one way of passing the time.

CHRIS. Yes, I've lost it. John says it comes back when I talk to my mother on the 'phone but I don't hear it.

LIBBY. I knew there was something I couldn't quite put my finger on. 'Our little Geordie.'

CHRIS. Who called me that?

LIBBY. John.

CHRIS. Not in my hearing. And not Geordie, Northumbrian.

LIBBY. I used to love it. Especially when you got really carried away and got broader and broader. Amongst all that RP it gave you a real flavour.

CHRIS. Not in Hexham. In Hexham the Queen's English was the voice you needed to go places. I wanted to talk what I'd been brought up to think was lovely.

LIBBY. People remembered you for it.

CHRIS. Not for what I said. What my voice said was where I came from and it wasn't foreign enough to be exotic. Hadrian's Wall not Blenheim or Chatsworth. A council estate in Hexham's not a great advert for England's green and pleasant land. It was remarked on in my civil service interview, I was commended for my French and Portuguese and the smattering of Arabic I'd picked up in my year in Oman, the criticism was reserved for my own. That's what I spent my time in the language lab doing. Learning what was supposed to be my own language. Learning it so I could understand the culture. A windy walk on the Sussex Downs. By coach to Canterbury Cathedral. A boat trip past the Mother of Parliaments to Hampton Court. A visit to Shakespeare's birth place.

LIBBY. Britain.

CHRIS. I thought that's what it was at the time. I wanted to be part of the foreign land. To belong in the way that John belongs. It's why I've never found being an ex-pat difficult. Even in England I was displaced. The only way you can explain Hexham is to say it's between London and Edinburgh. Life's easier as a chameleon.

LIBBY. Until you end up on a tartan carpet!

CHRIS. You have to try and lie on a stripe. To turn yourself into a straight line.

LIBBY. Can it be done? There are no straight lines in nature.

CHRIS. I try. John hates my background. I've a house in Putney – you have to, or you get left behind and there's nowhere to go back to. He wants me to move my mother there. She'd have nothing. No family, no friends. Wherever I move, I've at least got John.

LIBBY. Or John's got you.

CHRIS. I've got John.

LIBBY. I thought you were going to be Tessa.

Pause.

CHRIS. I'm not Tessa, not in a million years.

LIBBY. Did you know the two of them as a couple?

CHRIS. Only at Bristol. Not married. Rumours reached me of course.

LIBBY. Which were?

CHRIS. It worked well. It must have done, for John to marry again. Libby I'm not callous, but I'm grateful to Tessa for dying. For giving me my chance when I thought the chances had gone. I didn't think I'd be a family. I have to love Tess for that.

LIBBY. I hate George's first wife. I hate her for hurting him. I hate the way he waits to be hurt when all I am trying to do is live my life.

CHRIS. I'm in Tessa's debt. She even left me a child. My mother even agreed to board a plane so she could come to the wedding. I try my best to pay.

To give herself something to do she starts picking up and putting away LIBBY's *clothes.*

I was John's boss. I had the privilege of being able to look up his files, Tess would have made an ambassador's wife. She took to all this like a duck to water. She didn't have to think about hats and gloves. She could do them.

LIBBY. You wouldn't answer the question earlier.

CHRIS. I swapped the sea for a pond and the water's not quite the same.

We hear JOHN *outside.*

JOHN. Are you two going to gossip for ever?

CHRIS. Libby, I'm so glad it's you.

LIBBY. You can come in.

But even though he has heard this, JOHN *knocks.*
And so LIBBY *has to open the door.*

His dress proclaims that the evening is going to be fairly formal.

He carried his shoes and his cuffs are uncufflinked.

He walks straight up to CHRIS *and hands her the cufflinks so she can do his cuffs.*

She does them without comment.

He looks at the chaos.

JOHN. My first ambassador used to say chaos was the sign of an untidy mind. He'd not met you to be proved wrong.

LIBBY. I get the feeling I'm being complimented.

JOHN. I never did understand how you worked in your office.

LIBBY. I could, and still can always lay my hands on everything.

CHRIS. Darling, she needs a table. One of the ones from the cupboard on the landing.

JOHN. Can you get Yusef to clean these.

He gives her the shoes.

He exits

CHRIS. It would be as easy for him to take them downstairs himself. Or have two pairs then one would always be clean.

LIBBY. The other thing I remember about him at Bristol, his shoes were always clean.

CHRIS. Only in those days he cleaned them.

LIBBY *takes the towel from the mirror.*

He's much less changed than we are.

CHRIS. His has always been the same life. A straight line. He just 'is'.

LIBBY. It must be satisfying knowing what you want and getting it.

CHRIS. He won't get it. Ambassador to Washington at 45. He won't get it. He won't get Washington or Paris or Moscow or Rome or any of the big ones. Maybe one of the West Indies or Sweden or Holland or something – I'm his insurance on that.

LIBBY. Where did he blot his copy book?

CHRIS. Nowhere. He just hasn't got what it takes. He's not top rank.

LIBBY. Perhaps –

CHRIS. He won't.

LIBBY. What will he do?

CHRIS. I don't know. Say it will happen at 47, 50, wait. Then he'll retire and we'll go back to England.

LIBBY. There must be a lot.

CHRIS. Yes there are. And most of them would do better to get out and do something else.

LIBBY. Surely, he knows?

CHRIS. We pretend that he will. At least, I pretend. His father was a First Secretary. He wants to go beyond that. Believe me Libby, I'm not being disloyal but that is how it is.

LIBBY. You must love him a lot not to say.

CHRIS. That's the real diplomat in me. Me not telling him that Kit's bought him a Walkman for his birthday. Because I know John won't like it but if I tell him, he'll be too enthusiastic about being pleased. You know?

LIBBY. Yes. Being a wife's the best training you could get.

CHRIS. Qualify anyone for Washington!

JOHN (*from off*). Door, please.

Whoever can get there opens the door for him.

JOHN *enters with a table.*

JOHN. Where?

LIBBY. That's fine

JOHN *puts up the table.*

CHRIS. She can't have that. It's your modelling table.
It's got bits of glue all over it.

LIBBY. If you could give me a cloth or something. You still make models?

JOHN. I'm in the middle of Windsor Castle outer wall at the moment. I'd hoped to have a look round last time I was home but HM was installing Knights of the Garter.

LIBBY. He took me to Harlech to see the castle there. There was some problem about its dungeon.

CHRIS. You can't see the dungeons.

JOHN. They're still part of the structure. I'm afraid Harlech was one of the models sacked by Kit during his reign of terror.

LIBBY (*referring to the towel she's holding*). I'll return this to its proper place.

She picks up a couple of other bathroom items from her case and takes them and the towel into the bathroom.

CHRIS *and* JOHN *proceed to have a frantic and whispered conversation.*

CHRIS. You took her to Harlech?

JOHN. You know what it's like with a tape measure on your own.

CHRIS. Get a tape that doesn't retract.

JOHN. They still have to be held to the wall.

CHRIS. Why did you think it was me?

JOHN. We've done a lot of castles. She's not changed.

CHRIS. I think she has.

JOHN. Her clothes.

CHRIS. Well –

JOHN. Can't you drop a hint or something?

CHRIS. I suggested she had something ironed. Stoney ground.

JOHN. What does she think we have servants for?

CHRIS. Cleaning shoes?

JOHN. You think she'd make a bit of an effort.

CHRIS (*holding an outer garment and some underwear*). She wears that over this.

JOHN. I never did understand her. A three week trip, and she arrives with a holdall!

CHRIS. She goes places you can't get porters.

JOHN. Can't you lend her something?

CHRIS. No one's going to know apart from us.

JOHN. She only looks as if she's slept in them.

LIBBY *returns.*

JOHN. I'll leave you so you can finish dressing.
Shoes Christine.

Exit JOHN.

Pause.

CHRIS *looks at the shoes.*

CHRIS. Shoes, please, Christine. He thinks two pairs of shoes would be a waste of money. My money-conscious upbringing would say they'd take twice as long to wear out.

LIBBY. I can think of some aid groups who'd do well to adopt that logic.

CHRIS. He won't see it. I'll see you downstairs when you're ready.

LIBBY. I'm ready.

CHRIS. You've plenty of time to have a shower and get changed.

LIBBY. Is it smart?

CHRIS. I just think you might feel more comfortable.

LIBBY. Is this all in my honour?

CHRIS. Yes.

LIBBY. I don't need it.

CHRIS. We didn't know who you were. And people wanted to meet you.

LIBBY. Who would I let down if I didn't change?

CHRIS. Yourself.

LIBBY. Well, if it makes other people feel more comfortable. That's how we mastered the Empire. Dressing up and subduing the natives. I don't suppose those are the sort of comments to make here.

CHRIS. I must get these done or John will be greeting people in his socks. Just fill you in. The cocktails are so, when you meet people during the rest of the week, you've some idea about who each other is. Dinner's a chance for you to talk to people in more depth. You're sitting between Henry Thwaite and Marco Paillio.

LIBBY. Am I supposed to know who they are?

CHRIS. John's boss and the head of Fiat. Marco'll offer you the most wonderful discounts but remember it'll be left hand drive and the shipping costs from here will be prohibitive.

LIBBY. Why can't it just come from Italy?

CHRIS. His wife's local. He's got to keep the office open here in terms of his family commitment.

LIBBY. And John's boss?

There is a pause.

Say no more.

CHRIS. I haven't said anything.

LIBBY. I'd certainly better dress for John's boss.

CHRIS. I didn't say anything.

LIBBY. You speak the language like a native.

CHRIS. I always was good at languages!

LIBBY *goes into the bathroom with one of the things from the case.*

CHRIS *stands for a moment with the shoes.*

She exits.

Scene Three

CHRIS *and* JOHN'*s house. A reception room. It is furnished with things from the Property Services Agency. On display are various models of castles built by* JOHN. *It is after the cocktail party and after supper.*

Enter LIBBY *followed by* JOHN.

LIBBY *is in a furious mood.*

JOHN. Liz, I'm sorry.

LIBBY. I'm not!

JOHN. Look, I don't want to apologise for Henry but –

LIBBY. Then don't!

JOHN. I think you have to remember that he's –

LIBBY. Your boss, so you won't stand up to him?

JOHN. I think everyone understood that you've had a difficult time and you're tired.

LIBBY. You don't have to give me an excuse because I don't need one. Nor am I thinking of apologising. Not to you or anybody.

JOHN. Liz –

LIBBY. Libby, please. And if you've got any other dinner parties lined up for me cancel them, because the next time someone is outrageous I won't fight back I shall just walk out.

JOHN. You might have done better to walk out.

LIBBY. You'd only have tried to talk me back in.

JOHN. I understand the pressures –

LIBBY. Do you?

JOHN. Being away from home's hard work. And you've always been your own worst enemy.

LIBBY. That's not fair!

JOHN. You still enjoy picking an argument.

LIBBY. I didn't pick an argument!

JOHN. Yes, you did.

LIBBY. John, I did not pick an argument.

JOHN. Now you're picking an argument about whether you had an argument or not!

LIBBY. So I was supposed to sit there, say nothing, and let him get away with it? I've never let anybody do that John.

Pause.

I think I'll just go to bed.

JOHN. Christine is making us coffee.

LIBBY. Then accept that it was not because I was tired. Not

physically tired but tired of that sort of English man making those sort of jokes. Have you ever listened to him?

JOHN. Frequently, he's my senior.

LIBBY. And?

JOHN. In the real cut and thrust I find him very impressive.

LIBBY. Not at dinner?

JOHN. Dinner's a very different situation.

LIBBY. What if I'd been somebody that mattered. Somebody important?

JOHN. All our guests are important.

LIBBY. A woman diplomat from abroad?

JOHN. That's asking him to behave as if you're something you're not.

LIBBY. That's precisely my point.

JOHN. Libby, I agree but –

LIBBY. Then you don't agree. But?

JOHN. We wanted to make it as informal as possible.

LIBBY. And tonight was Henry's definition of informal?

JOHN. In other circumstances he might have behaved with more discretion. I'm sorry, perhaps I shouldn't have introduced you as an old friend. He assumed that made you one of us.

LIBBY. I wasn't allowed to be one of you.

JOHN. You were saved 20 years of Henry and his ilk.

LIBBY. And watching you grow more and more like them.

JOHN. A diplomat represents his country not himself.

LIBBY. Doesn't yourself count?

Pause.

Does Christine know?

JOHN. No.

LIBBY. Did Tess?

JOHN. I don't know. Does George?

LIBBY. Some. You did change me.

JOHN. I'm flattered.

LIBBY. You never believed in change for the better! Didn't Tessa ask?

JOHN. Tessa got what she wanted.

LIBBY. Which was marriage?

JOHN. I wanted to marry Tess. And Liz, neither did I ever regret it.

Pause.

LIBBY. Libby.

She looks at one of the models.

Concentric?

JOHN *comes and stands beside her.*

JOHN. Motte and bailey with an outer curtain.

LIBBY. Does the drawbridge work?

JOHN. Of course.

He winds it down for her,

Up?

LIBBY. It's your toy.

JOHN *winds the drawbridge up.*

I suppose the real contemporary imperialists are the rocket builders.

CHRIS *enters with the tray of coffee.*

How does he carry them round the world without breaking them?

CHRIS. The embassy packers. Their repertoire is astonishing. Wood shavings. Polystyrene chips. Shredded paper.

LIBBY. Embassy shredded?

CHRIS. Good God, no. And thank God I don't have to dust

them. If we get a home posting we are going to get a cleaning lady for that very purpose.

JOHN. So she tells me.

LIBBY. Where will you live?

JOHN. Oxford
CHRIS. Putney } *Together*

Pause.

CHRIS. Coffee?

LIBBY. Lovely.

CHRIS. It's dried milk reconstituted I'm afraid.

LIBBY. That's all right.

CHRIS (*to* JOHN *to explain*). I just didn't have the time.

LIBBY pours the milk and spills it.

LIBBY. I'm sorry.

CHRIS. I'll get a cloth.

JOHN. Ring?

CHRIS. I've sent them to bed –

JOHN. They're supposed to stay until –

CHRIS. I know when they are supposed to stay until. But they do have lives and homes of their own.

She goes out.

JOHN comes and sits on the sofa next to LIBBY.

They look at each other.

They wait for CHRIS *to return.*

Finally LIBBY *sits forward to drink her coffee.*

There is a photograph of KIT *on the coffee table.*

LIBBY picks it up.

LIBBY. He's the spit!

More silence.

She looks at the photograph.

JOHN. Oh, bloody hell. Christine was supposed to remind me. He'll be in bed.

JOHN *gets up again.*

JOHN. You must give us a list of what you'd like to see while you're here. We've marked sightseeing in for Saturday.

She puts the photo back on the table.

LIBBY. I'm in your hands. But no dungeons. Do you know I won't take visitors round Harlech Castle any more, we go there so often.

JOHN. We thought we might have a picnic.

LIBBY. Anything's fine by me. But I'm not a great sightseer, you know that.

JOHN. I'd hoped there'd been a change for the better.

CHRIS *comes back with a cloth.*

She mops up the milk.

She is about to go back to the kitchen with the cloth.

LIBBY. Oh, don't take it back.

CHRIS. Are you thinking of spilling the lot! There's a beautiful moon, you should see it on the Nile.

She goes back out.

JOHN *opens veranda doors for* LIBBY.

LIBBY *goes out.*

LIBBY. It is beautiful.

JOHN. We ought to take you night riding in the desert. Christine won't come, she never learned to ride.

The telephone rings.

Those are Henry's manners, he rings as soon as he gets in to thank us.

LIBBY. And he can tell you what he really thinks of me without me overhearing!

JOHN. Excuse me.

He should fractionally touch her.

He goes to answer the phone.

LIBBY *goes further onto the veranda.*

We go back in time.

The room becomes smaller.

There is university party music.

A farewell party is being given by CHRISTINE.

I suspect the music is Simon and Garfunkel stuff.

CHRIS, *in 1969 clothes, comes into the room.*

She carries a plate of sausage rolls and a bottle of wine.

Her accent in the scene is noticeably broader Northumbrian.

She's busy making the party run smoothly.

She empties ash trays and plumps cushions, perhaps throwing a couple on floor for that Bohemian atmosphere.

She puts down the wine and sausage rolls. She takes a guitar out of the cupboard. She takes the guitar next door.

She comes back for the sausage rolls.

LIBBY *comes in. She has a glass of wine and is in sixties clothes.* CHRIS *immediately picks up the sausage rolls and offers her one.*

CHRIS. No one next door seems interested in sausage rolls. I think it's once people start drinking.

LIBBY. I won't.

CHRIS. I didn't buy them. My mother sent them. From Hexham.

Then she's embarrassed by this admission and puts them and the wine down on the table.

LIBBY. They'll miss you.

CHRIS. Yes. I'll miss them.

LIBBY. You know I think you should stay here and do your MA. If you wanted to go straight on to a doctorate, I'd support that.

CHRIS. It's only a year.

LIBBY. I think you're wasted as an *au-pair*.

CHRIS. It's the chance of a lifetime. I'd be daft – silly, not to take it.

LIBBY. And then what?

CHRIS. The Spicer's were very good to me in Portugal, I got invited to parties and everything. And I must have given satisfaction or they'd not have asked me to go to Muscat with them. Their friends were very interesting people. I even met MP's. And I've got my ticket and everything now.

LIBBY. Don't waste yourself.

CHRIS. Ethne Spicer and I are going to learn Arabic together. She says the embassy will pay. She doesn't treat you like a servant and I'm good with the children. And it's only the little ones apart from when Piers comes back from boarding school.

LIBBY. Promise me you'll come back when your year's up.

CHRIS. You can't promise can you?

LIBBY. Don't just go and get married.

CHRIS. What's wrong with getting married?

LIBBY. Don't let it be your be all and end all.

CHRIS. I'd like to be married with a husband and children. Women who don't get married – well, they're odd aren't they? No one to do anything for. I don't mean you. I mean 27 isn't old these days is it. And they always say Mr Right happens when you stop looking for him.

JOHN *enters. He is at the party in a suit.*

LIBBY. Here he is.

JOHN. Who is?

LIBBY. You?

CHRIS. This side's pork and this side's beef.

She hold the plate of sausage rolls out to JOHN.

JOHN. You've done us proud.

He takes one.

CHRIS. I think it's nice to have food at a party. I'll just see if anybody next door –

JOHN. Oh, Christine –

He takes some academic magazine out of his pocket.

CHRIS. Oh, you remembered. Thank you.

She takes the magazine from him.

JOHN. It's –

He takes the magazine back from her and turns it to a certain page.

He says to explain to LIBBY.

Fraser's article.

CHRIS *is looking at it.*

CHRIS. He hasn't even given me a footnote!

JOHN. No.

CHRIS. It's, it's so – he's abusing his position! These are my ideas! He's even used my chapter heading!

LIBBY. Can I see?

CHRIS *hands the magazine to* LIBBY.

CHRIS. It's an abuse of his position Liz.

LIBBY. I'm sure it wasn't conscious.

CHRIS. I'm sure it was.

JOHN. At least it means you can relax about tomorrow.

CHRIS. Why does it?

JOHN. He'll give you credit.

CHRIS. No he won't. He'll just say I've regurgitated his ideas. His ideas which were my ideas in the first place!

LIBBY (*handing back the magazine*). You could make a case for plagiarism.

CHRIS. I will.

JOHN. You could ask them to publish an erratum.

CHRIS. Demand!

LIBBY. In the long run is it really going to matter?

CHRIS. One, Fraser's abusing his position as professor which means he gets away with hoovering up all his students ideas. Two, it was the liberal response to Napoleon which I was going to use as the basis of my MA.

LIBBY. He'll be flattered if that's your MA.

CHRIS. Forgive me Liz, but am I here for my teachers so they can teach me, or am I here for myself so I can learn?

LIBBY. You know what my response to that is going to be.

CHRIS. So you'll take it up with Fraser?

LIBBY. Well –

Pause.

I'm in a difficult position.

CHRIS. You won't?

JOHN. Chris, you're being unfair on Liz.

CHRIS. No, John, I am not.

LIBBY. In the world of ideas, plariarism is very difficult to prove.

CHRIS. That's going to be it, isn't it? The random idea that floated in!

LIBBY. We all know about Fraser –

CHRIS. *We* do. What about other people reading this? My parents wouldn't understand it, but if they had my name on it they'd read it. He (*meaning* JOHN) thought it was by me.

JOHN. That's why I noticed it. I was sort of flicking through and I thought 'Christine kept this quiet'.

CHRIS. Well, I'm not going to keep quiet.

LIBBY. It won't matter in Muscat.

CHRIS. Fraser is not going to get away with it. I'm not like John, I don't want glory from the world but I would like credit.

She thrusts the plate of sausage rolls under JOHN's *nose.*

JOHN *takes a sausage roll.*

JOHN. Go on Chris. Fight.

CHRIS. Don't worry, I will. I'm going to sausage roll next door
and then I am going to lock myself in the toilet and read this
properly.

JOHN *takes a biro out of his pocket.*

JOHN. Take notes.

CHRIS. Thank you.

She takes the biro and goes.

LIBBY. Chris doesn't believe in making life easy for herself!

JOHN. It's that tough northerner in 'er. You've got to admit
she's right.

He looks at the sausage roll.

JOHN. It's like being at some hideous sort of wedding
reception!

LIBBY. She's gone to such a lot of effort.

JOHN. You think with her brain that she wouldn't bother. That
she'd just get on with being clever and leave it at that. And not
worry about all the little homely things.

LIBBY. Like me?

JOHN. Tess for domesticity, you for sex and –

LIBBY. Intellectual stimulation?

JOHN. That's what I was going to suggest for Christine. If you
could get her to use the word lavatory. But then she wouldn't
be our little Geordie, would she?

He looks at the sausage roll.

I wonder if the beef ones are better?

JOHN *puts the sausage roll in an ash tray.*

JOHN. Shut your eyes and hold out your hands.

LIBBY. I haven't seen you for three weeks!

JOHN. And whose fault is that?

LIBBY. I had exam papers to mark.

JOHN. Do as you're told whilst the little Geordie is force-feeding them next door.

So LIBBY *does as she is told.*

Out of his pockets JOHN *takes handfuls of shells and also something like a lipstick or something which* TESSA *has given him to put in his pocket.*

LIBBY. Harlech beach!

She opens her eyes.

JOHN. My pockets are full of sand.

He turns the sand on to the floor.

She'll be vacuuming in the morning.

LIBBY. I'm sure Christine does the vacuuming before she goes to bed.

JOHN. Because she doesn't have anything to go to bed for.

I had great difficulty explaining to Tess that I'd turned into a nature lover.

LIBBY *picks out the lipstick.*

LIBBY. Can't Tessa carry her own bits and pieces?

JOHN. Sorry.

He takes the lipstick back.

LIBBY. They don't look the same do they?

JOHN *takes one of the shells, spits on it and rubs it with his finger.*

JOHN. There you are.

But she can't take it because her hands are full of the other shells.

JOHN *holds it up to her ear.*

Can you hear the sound of the sea.

LIBBY. Tremadoc Bay.

He kisses her. Not a big kiss.

JOHN. Tell me how I did?

LIBBY. I can't!

He kisses her again.

JOHN. Yes you can.

LIBBY. John!

JOHN. I'll know tomorrow.

LIBBY. What if somebody comes in?

JOHN. There's nothing to come in for. All the food and alcohol is next door.

At this moment CHRIS *enters to retrieve the wine.*

She still has the magazine under her arm.

CHRIS. Sorry!

LIBBY. I was listening to the sound of the sea!

CHRIS. It's not the sea. It's the sound of your blood pumping that you actually hear.

She takes the wine, noticing the sausage roll.

Was there something wrong?

JOHN. I dropped it.

CHRIS. I'll bring you another.

JOHN. I'll come and get one.

CHRIS. They're on the table under Che Guevara.

She goes out.

LIBBY *stuffs the shells into pockets – she's probably wearing a trouser suit.*

LIBBY. A man is coming to ask me questions about you tomorrow afternoon.

JOHN. Yes.

LIBBY. You knew?

JOHN. You were a reference.

LIBBY. What's he going to ask?

JOHN. You're the academic reference.

LIBBY. You're supposed to ask!

JOHN. You'd have said no.

LIBBY. Do you really think joining the foreign service is a way of doing good in the world?

JOHN. I believe in my country.

LIBBY. It's exactly the same as Edward the First building castles to subdue the Welsh!

JOHN. The more fortunate have their part to play.

LIBBY. Do you think I don't know what you're doing by using me as a reference?

JOHN. Take out the opposition before they can take you out.

He kisses her.

When the kiss breaks.

LIBBY. I'm good with flowers and I can play tennis and ride a horse and I'm sure if you got posted to an embassy with French windows –

JOHN. It's a job where wives are important.

LIBBY. Meaning she has to believe in what you're doing?

JOHN. Yes. You're the one who won't be convinced.

LIBBY. You could change your mind.

JOHN. Liz, it's what I've always been going to do.

LIBBY. What if your government asked you to do something you didn't believe in?

JOHN. I'd believe in my government. And the people like you, who elect the government.

LIBBY. I shall expect a postcard when you get to Washington.

JOHN. You'll get an invite.

She breaks away from him.

LIBBY. I'm jealous.

JOHN. You've got nothing to be jealous of.

LIBBY. Haven't I?

JOHN. Tess is waiting for marriage.

LIBBY. And Tess would be the right sort of wife. Would I count against you?

JOHN. You prove I'm not a homosexual.

LIBBY. Let's go!

JOHN. We can't.

LIBBY. We could do our meeting on the corner trick.

JOHN. Let's save it for tomorrow. For after the results. Unless you want to spill the beans now.

Pause.

You know I can keep a secret.

Pause.

Please Liz.

LIBBY. I don't have any beans to spill.

JOHN. Go on.

LIBBY. I don't.

JOHN. The marks must be all decided.

LIBBY. They aren't.

JOHN. What are they playing at?

LIBBY. There are still some we haven't agreed on.

JOHN. Do you mean mine's not agreed on?

LIBBY. No.

JOHN. No it's not agreed on or no it's agreed on?

LIBBY. I had to leave the examiner's meeting.

JOHN. For the sake of this?

LIBBY. Because I had to declare an interest in you. I'm not an uninterested party.

JOHN. So you've walked out and left Fraser and the like to carve me up! Fraser, whose only response to a good idea is to steal it. Cite our hostess's essay on the liberal response to Napoleon.

LIBBY. There's no argument over Christine.

Silence

You aren't supposed to know that.

JOHN. She doesn't need a first like I do!

LIBBY. Even you realise she deserves it.

JOHN. She'll only go off and get married.

LIBBY. Which is exactly what you're planning – isn't it?

JOHN. I was relying on you.

Pause.

LIBBY. Have I really fallen for that one?

JOHN. No, you haven't.

LIBBY. Honestly?

JOHN. Honestly. But I thought you'd be on my side.

LIBBY. I am.

JOHN. Declaring an interest hardly makes you sound fair!

LIBBY. Doesn't it?

JOHN. They're not going to think you've been objective, are they?

LIBBY. I wanted to give them the benefit of the doubt.

JOHN. What's Tess got?

LIBBY. Let's not have this conversation.

JOHN. You don't think I can keep a secret from Tess?

Pause.

Sorry, that was below the belt.

LIBBY. She hasn't thrown up any surprises.

JOHN. A 2.2?

LIBBY. I didn't tell you.

JOHN. Did you declare an interest?

LIBBY. There was no discussion. She did exactly what was expected. A steady 2.2 on all papers.

JOHN. Which bugger marked me down?

LIBBY. Does having a first matter that much?

JOHN. Yes, if you've promised yourself an embassy at 45.

LIBBY. What if you don't?

JOHN. I'm not second division and I'm not going to settle for it.

LIBBY. I don't see how I can help.

JOHN. So who? Which paper?

LIBBY *is silent.*

Ireland?

She stands silent.

Twentieth-century interpretations of the constitution?

Nothing.

There is a long pause.

LIBBY. Have you worked it out?

JOHN. Why?

LIBBY. It was a bad paper.

JOHN. Who says?

LIBBY. I marked it.

JOHN. So you say it was a bad paper?

LIBBY. I'm supposed to be your goddamn tutor.

JOHN. You're supposed to be impartial.

LIBBY. Do you know how hard I tried to be fair? You didn't answer the question.

JOHN. Of course I did!

LIBBY. You totally ignored the social factors involved in the collapse of the third republic.

JOHN. I got the economics right.

LIBBY. People, you forgot the people! It wasn't an integrated essay.

JOHN. The third republic had never heard of Karl Marx!

LIBBY. Read the question. Answer the question. But I should have realised that you never do.

JOHN. So finally you take revenge!

LIBBY. Do you think I didn't want you to do well?
First time through I thought whatever I feel about this candidate it's not going to influence me. Like my mother not trying to give away the fact that I am her favourite by making sure I get just that bit less.

JOHN. A lot less.

LIBBY. Then I said to myself, 'Okay, Liz you've bent too far over backwards.' Be on his side. So I marked it again.

JOHN. And how many marks did you find me?

LIBBY. Three.

JOHN. How many did I need?

LIBBY. I thought, I'm tired. I haven't seen him since we went to Harlech. I marked it again. One.

JOHN. I don't believe you.

LIBBY. You don't believe you're capable of doing a bad paper?

JOHN. You knew how important it was.

LIBBY. What did you want me to do? Cheat. Do you think it didn't hurt me?

JOHN. I thought you were on my side.

LIBBY. I was.

Pause.

That's why I left. I thought you stood a better chance of having your marks argued up without me there. I let the other examiners think what they like. What they'll think is that I'm bitter and jealous and therefore grudge you marks.

JOHN. Isn't it true?

LIBBY. If letting everyone think that is the best I can do for you, let them think it. Let them discuss my life and find it wanting. Let them laugh at the lecturer throwing herself at one of her students. Because that's what they'll do. And I'll never quite be trusted over the attractive ones again.

JOHN. So what am I going to get?

They look at each other.

CHRIS *comes in.*

She has half a grapefruit with cheese and grapes on sticks stuck in it.

She's still got the magazine under her arm.

CHRIS. Ellie is going to sing.

She puts the magazine away in something.

I think I'm going to have to forget about reading it until everyone's gone.

She thrusts the grapefruit between them.

At home we call it hedgehog. You have to be careful. The sticks are a bit sharp.

They decline.

No one seems hungry. I think it's because tomorrow's the big day.

JOHN. If you want my help against Fraser.

CHRIS. It's very kind of you.

JOHN. We wouldn't want them to get away with it, would we.

CHRIS. No.

LIBBY. You'll make a good diplomat John.

JOHN. Thank you. Stick in there, Christine.

He makes some gesture to her.

CHRIS. If I do need your help, I'll get in touch.

JOHN. I wasn't going to tell you this because I just wanted you to see it in print. I did send the editor a letter. Tessa and I thought that might be quite cheery for you sitting in Muscat.

CHRIS. That was nice.

JOHN. Tess is worried about you being lonely.

CHRIS. I don't suppose I will be after a bit. And it's only a year and then I come home.

JOHN. If you'll excuse me. You'll understand, there's a question I have to ask Tessa tonight.

JOHN goes.

CHRIS. I was wondering how I was going to get everybody in my address book.

The two women watch him go.

CHRIS. Lucky Tessa.

LIBBY. Do you think so?

CHRIS. He just knows how to do the right thing.

LIBBY. Christine, I have to go.

CHRIS. Was there –

LIBBY. No, it's a lovely party. And that looks ever such fun. I'm exhausted with marking.

CHRIS. You look tired.

LIBBY. Good luck.

CHRIS. Thank you. And you.

LIBBY. Thanks.

CHRIS. And thank you.

LIBBY. You understand about my problem with Fraser?

CHRIS. An acknowledgement would have been enough. Just so my parents could see it wasn't all wasted.

LIBBY. Yes, I understand.

Christine looks at the grapefruit.

I'll see myself out.

CHRIS. It's a bit of a waste of grapefruit really.

She takes it next door.

LIBBY *prepares to leave.*

She feels in her pockets.

She finds the shells.

She throws them away.

She empties the sand from her pockets.

There are suddenly whoops and cries from next door of 'John' *and* 'Tess' *and* 'Congratulations'.

LIBBY *stands for a moment.*

She has gone cold all over.

She takes one shell and with immense dignity, which costs her everything, she leaves.

ACT TWO

Scene One

CHRIS *and* JOHN's *house. The reception room.* CHRIS *comes back from returning the cloth to the kitchen.*

LIBBY *comes in from the veranda.*

LIBBY. Christine, I'm sorry. After all the trouble you'd gone to. I didn't mean it to turn into a scene.

CHRIS. Least said, soonest mended.

LIBBY. I thought Henry'd see the funny side. And it was about time someone else made a joke.

CHRIS. Honestly Libby.

LIBBY. I know you warned me but –

CHRIS. Henry hasn't been in England, except for leave, in 12 years.

LIBBY. You and John are both making excuses for him!

JOHN *comes back in.*

JOHN. I swear to you that child comes from a different planet –

CHRIS. John, I'm sorry!

LIBBY. I thought I was being picked over.

JOHN. I was trying to salvage my relationship with my twin sister whose bottom line seems to be that she's never going to have Kit to stay again.

(*To* LIBBY.) Do you honestly think it's too much to ask? To have her nephew for one night?

CHRIS. It's more than that.

JOHN. It's only ever one night at a time. It's not as if there are dozens of other family commitments clamouring for her attention. You think by now she'd have realised there are responsibilities beyond herself.

LIBBY. He is your son.

CHRIS. The two of them are like red rags to bulls.

LIBBY. If he was my child, Vee would be the last person I'd want to leave him with. Unless she's changed a lot.

JOHN. She's got religion.

LIBBY. Veronica?

JOHN. Is that any stranger than you suddenly deciding to become a doctor?

LIBBY. I became a doctor to try and change things.

CHRIS. Vee looks on religion in much the same way.

JOHN. Threatening to throw a child out on the streets is heardly Christian!

CHRIS. What did he do?

JOHN. He wouldn't pray. I ask you, is that too much to ask to keep the peace?

CHRIS. If he doesn't believe –

JOHN. He could have got away with a few mumblings.

LIBBY. It's a bit hypocritical.

JOHN. He just has to oil the wheels.

CHRIS. I don't think Vee should force him.

JOHN. Do you want to take him to England every time he has to go back to school?

LIBBY. At 14 couldn't he do it on his own?

JOHN. Thirteen.

LIBBY. Surely –

JOHN. You don't have children Liz, you don't understand the responsibilities.

LIBBY. Libby –

Pause.

CHRIS. How do you know Vee?

LIBBY. Bristol.

CHRIS. I never met her at Bristol.

JOHN. You must have done, darling.

LIBBY. She always wore black. Does she still?

JOHN. She consider women priests the devil incarnate.

LIBBY. What's she looking for?

CHRIS. She thinks you can be happy after you're dead.

JOHN. That's not exactly –

CHRIS. Yes, she does.

LIBBY. Chris, you must have known Vee at Bristol.

CHRIS. What was she doing?

JOHN. She used to infuriate Tessa by turning up for parties.

  CHRIS *shakes her head*.

JOHN. Christine didn't go in much for parties.

CHRIS. I did.

JOHN. You were always too busy burrowing away getting your degree.

CHRIS. You and Tess were too busy being loves' young dream to notice me. That's not fair, you did write to the editor of *Historical Debate*.

JOHN. Thank you! Vee used to sit moping about at home telling the parent's how much she missed me. Then one or the other of them would give in to this touching show of filial affection and give her the train fare up. She'd hitch and blow it all in the union bar.

CHRIS. You never told me that bit.

JOHN. I was supposed to be introducing her to suitable men, I did my best and she worked through the lot to no avail. By which time mother had spent a fortune on trains and clothes. Well Kit's going to have to apologise to her.

LIBBY. I'm sorry. It was my fault.

  Pause.

  If I'd held my peace.

CHRIS. He might still have not remembered!

LIBBY. And Christine did warn me – in a manner of speaking –

JOHN. Libby, you have to remember there are things on which Chris and Henry don't quite see eye to eye.

CHRIS. Don't see eye to knee-cap!

JOHN. Actually just don't see!

LIBBY. It's just if Henry is supposed to be representing our interests in the world –

JOHN. British interests.

LIBBY. I am British and he ought to know what our interests are. For Henry, women are on a par with the Welsh!

JOHN. I think if you'd got to know him you'd have found him very well informed.

LIBBY. He's certainly not that on the way I got all my brains in my pretty little head. When I tell him exactly, as neurologically and physiologically accurately as I can – I am accused of being clever – which I thought was the purpose of brains in the first place – and trying to put him down.

JOHN. That wasn't what he meant, was it?

LIBBY. What did he mean?

JOHN. It was –

He looks at CHRIS.

It was a compliment. He didn't mean anything by it. At least that's not what he meant.

LIBBY. I know what he meant.

JOHN. Then why did you say what you did?

LIBBY. I was answering a question.

JOHN. But that wasn't the question.

LIBBY. It was the question I heard –

JOHN. Liz, you're too clever to –

LIBBY. Yes?

JOHN. Clever women also like to know they're attractive.

LIBBY. John, whatever I see when I look in a mirror, it's not pretty.

JOHN. Attractive. Charming. Fetching.

LIBBY *says nothing.*

Okay, no compliments.

LIBBY. Try me on clever.

JOHN. You were deliverately provocative, Liz.

CHRIS. Libby.

JOHN. I meant Libby.

LIBBY. I answered a question which was put to me.

JOHN. In a completely different spirit.

LIBBY. The spirit in which I took it.

JOHN. For God's sake why? Couldn't you just let it ride?

LIBBY. No.

JOHN. We were having a perfectly pleasant dinner.

LIBBY. I wasn't.

JOHN. That was because you were deliberately provocative to keep yourself amused.

LIBBY. No one else was amusing me!

She turns to CHRIS.

I thought you'd be on my side.

JOHN. Perhaps Christine –

LIBBY. Couldn't you see what he was doing.

CHRIS. Henry's asked me if I'd go to Tunis.

JOHN. Pardon?

CHRIS. They need somebody there. Do you remember, we talked about it this afternoon?

JOHN. Henry and I talked about it this afternoon but he gave no indication –

LIBBY. Congratulations!

CHRIS. I've asked for time to think.

JOHN. He didn't ask me.

CHRIS. He knows you're tied up.

JOHN. He might at least have asked me what I thought!

LIBBY. What would you have thought?

CHRIS. I'm sorry Libby.

LIBBY. Now at least I understand why.

CHRIS. So little of one's life is one's own!

JOHN. Do you want to go?

CHRIS. I don't know. Do I want to go?

LIBBY. I think the two of you should discuss this without me.

She gets up.

CHRIS. I think you were right. I supported you all the way. Erica and I would have liked to have applauded.

Pause.

LIBBY. Thank you. Good night.

JOHN. 'Night.

CHRIS. There's bottled water by your bed and in the bathroom.

LIBBY. Thank you.

She exits.

Pause.

CHRIS. I'm sorry I forgot to remind you about Kit. Henry's offer's rather swept me off my feet.

JOHN. It's my own fault. I should have remembered. Well I think we can guess about Nairobi. Just because you're a feminist, it doesn't mean you can't have manners.

CHRIS. Where were Henry's manners?

JOHN. Darling, everybody knows, he's just like that.

CHRIS. Why can't he change?

JOHN. People put up with it when it suits them.

CHRIS. You can't expect me not to consider it seriously. I'd find out if it was what I wanted. Six months. You could take your leave in Tunis. Each bit would be ten weeks at most.

JOHN. You've obviously made up your mind.

CHRIS. I haven't made up my mind.

JOHN. You've already rearranged my leave.

CHRIS. I've been trying to solve the problem.

JOHN. Then you've decided to go.

CHRIS. No, I'm asking you.

JOHN. I was looking forward to showing you Devon.

CHRIS. Devon will be there next year.

JOHN. They'll have done the time share conversion on Nun's Croft.

CHRIS. I never knew it when you lived there. You could have three weeks in England instead of six.

JOHN. Christine, you decide and then we'll sort it out.

CHRIS. I want you to want me not to want to go and I want you to want me to go. I used to be able to think!

JOHN. Don't be stupid Christine. Of course you can think.

CHRIS. Not when I don't know what I want!

JOHN. Then perhaps you should go and find out what you do want. If it's only six months.

CHRIS. Do we have six months?

JOHN. No, I don't think we do.

Pause.

Do we?

CHRIS. No.

Pause.

I could come back.

JOHN. Yes, you could. But I'd have to know why. Whether you'd come back because you've served your time. Or because

I was here and you're married to me. Or just because it's home and when you open the wardrobe it will have your clothes inside.

CHRIS. I haven't got another wardrobe.

JOHN. There are several in Putney that will be yours from September.

CHRIS. It isn't home.

Pause.

I don't even know where I come from any more.

JOHN. Perhaps that's why you need to go.

CHRIS. It's a job somebody's got to do.

JOHN. You're being offered it because you're expedient.

CHRIS. I know that.

JOHN. Don't you mind?

CHRIS. I've always been expedient. As a woman in this game it's your only asset.

JOHN. Christine, of course I don't want you to go. I want you here. I need you here. What do I know about cooking asparagus?

It's the fatal thing to say.

CHRIS. You bloody steam it.

JOHN. Thank you.

The telephone rings.

Right on cue.

CHRIS. He'll be furious he couldn't get through because you were talking to London.

JOHN. You'd better go and tell him.

CHRIS *gets up.*

CHRIS. I wish I'd stood up for Libby before I said yes.

The phone stops.

Together they count.

One, two, three, four, five, six, seven, eight, nine, ten, eleven, twelve, thirteen, fourteen, fifteen –

They wait.

The phone rings.

There is one of those shared moments that makes it so difficult.

JOHN. Isn't it consoling that he thinks he might have dialled the wrong number?

CHRIS. He'll blame the damn wops at the exchange!

CHRIS exists to answer the phone.

John does window closing.

He puts his hand into one of the castles and crushes it.

Not a big gesture.

He turns off the lights.

He crosses the room in darkness picking up the coffee things as he goes.

Scene Two

Brilliant sunlight.

The desert. A shadow is cast by a large statue that we can't see. A picnic rug has been put down where it was obviously in the shade, but the shade has now moved. The shade will have moved again by the end of the scene.

Enter LIBBY. She wears the crease-resistant dress. It is creased. She looks up at the statue, shielding her eyes from the sun. But she realises it's really too hot. She sits down on the rug. It is the rug that she and JOHN made love on, on Harlech Beach. Then she realises that the rug is not in the shade. She throws it up a couple of times to get it straight and puts it down in the shade.

She lies down on the rug.

JOHN *enters.*

He stands above her for a moment

She opens her eyes and looks at him. Shading her eyes from the sun.

JOHN. Perhaps you'll find it more interesting with the guide book.

LIBBY. Too closed in and dark. You promised me no dungeons!

JOHN. They aren't dungeons they're tombs.

LIBBY. That's why I never liked the dungeons.

JOHN. Would you rather go back?

LIBBY. Not at all.

JOHN. Then perhaps we should go on to the Serapeum.

LIBBY. If you want.

JOHN. I think it's one of the most interesting tombs, it only came to light in –

But LIBBY'*s interest is on something in the sand.*

JOHN *bends down to look at it.*

A dung beetle.

LIBBY. Living on excrement.

JOHN. They believed they held the secret of eternal life.

LIBBY. Why?

JOHN. They thought they were only male.

LIBBY. Don't you believe in the future?

JOHN. You know I do.

LIBBY. One day George will die and I will be left all alone.

Pause.

JOHN. You think that at the time. I found Christine.

LIBBY. Will you miss her?

JOHN. Yes.

LIBBY. She's lucky to get another chance.

JOHN. The FO's lucky to get her back.

LIBBY. Perhaps that's what I meant. The two of you should be having this time together.

JOHN. She's a lot to arrange. And I could hardly not bring you to see the sights.

LIBBY. Even though I'm not particularly interested?

JOHN. It gives us a little time on our own without people clamouring for our attention. And Christine did this whole shebang last week with Kit. I thought it was one of the things she enjoyed. I don't think I could see the pyramids too often.

LIBBY. It's just the enclosed spaces, that feeling of being trapped. You don't feel it, do you?

JOHN. Never have.

LIBBY. I used to think about you every day.

JOHN. And then?

LIBBY. It's odd things that remind me. Someone walking in the street and I think – and it's not. And if it wasn't for you I wouldn't have quit Bristol, I wouldn't have done VSO, I wouldn't have met George and I wouldn't be here now.

JOHN. Did you tell him you knew who I was?

LIBBY *shakes her head.*

LIBBY. It wouldn't have been fair. When I heard about Kit I wanted the earth to open and swallow me. I'd been to Nigeria and sloughed off some of my pain there, but that bit of the new skin wasn't thick enough. I walked out on the ice on a pond and waited for it to break.

JOHN. Sometimes we all need a sign.

LIBBY. George found me. Having got to the centre I couldn't get back. He came and carried me. Two of us and the ice still didn't break. He's carried me ever since. He was taking a walk and I was looking for the answer to my life. And I ended up being the answer to his life.

She rolls over and plays with the fringe of the rug.

Do you think French car rugs are as specific to the French as tartan ones are to the British?

JOHN. I don't know.

LIBBY. I'm surprised we didn't wear it out.

JOHN. I don't think that's what my parents intended it for.

LIBBY. Did your parents have no imagination?

JOHN. You've always been there. Do you know that?

LIBBY. Did you do anything differently?

JOHN. You reproached me a lot. Looked over my shoulder.

LIBBY. But everything is exactly the same.

JOHN. Is it?

LIBBY. You're exactly what you said you were going to be.

JOHN. I won't get Washington.

LIBBY. How do you know?

JOHN. I'm not good enough.

LIBBY. You're not 45 yet!

JOHN. Christine was the flier. She went in two years behind me
and still ended up in front. I envy her being as good as she is,
her facility with languages is extraordinary.

Pause.

I never felt I did deserve her. I've always known she'd see
through me and go. I sometimes think a stupid woman has a
lot more options.

LIBBY. We make ourselves stupid, so we don't have them.

JOHN. I believed that she believed that I was what she wanted
to make her happy. We have a game about a dinner party we
hold in Washington. But we won't ever have it. But to put up
with what you do have to put up with, not seeing home, not
seeing Kit, some weeks hardly seeing Christine, you do have
to believe that you'll do it. And one day you realise that you
can see the stick and the string and the carrot. You realise
who's the donkey. But you're so used to seeing the carrot, the
string and the stick that you go on seeing them. She chose
between careers. How can I not let her take her chance?

LIBBY. Is it supposed to be my fault? Because you didn't get
your first-class degree?

JOHN. No Liz, you mustn't think that. Promise me you won't think that.

He grabs her.

Promise me.

She just looks at him.

I'm trying to say sorry!

He breaks from her.

LIBBY. Then say it!

He cannot.

Did you know I was pregnant?

JOHN. Harlech?

LIBBY. We were both reckless.

JOHN. You aren't now?

LIBBY. That was always supposed to be a secret.

JOHN. Then why tell?

LIBBY. So you knew.

JOHN. Why do I need to know?

LIBBY. So you know there could have been another one of you that wasn't Kit.

JOHN. I love Kit. Whatever the disappointments about him, I love him. He's not what I wanted him to be. But how can I blame him when I'm not what I wanted to be?

LIBBY. It's the hardest thing to fight in my job, the expectation not being fulfilled. If we have a lot of children one will come up good. Why do you think I took up family planning? I wanted people to have the right to that easier choice.

JOHN. Are you sorry?

LIBBY. You have to forgive yourself.

JOHN. But not me?

Long, long, pause.

LIBBY. I thought that's what I was coming here to do. No. That would be hurting George. He's a better man than that.

JOHN. I'm glad you have someone you deserve.

LIBBY. He would never hurt me. He never kissed my toes.

JOHN. Perhaps not in the same way.

LIBBY. Never. I meet you in the most unlikely places and for reasons that I can't work out.

JOHN. We'll go on meeting all our lives.

LIBBY. Yes. What did you think had happened to me?

JOHN. I hoped you were happy. I didn't want it to be my fault if you weren't.

LIBBY. I envy Vee God. It must be nice to think someone else can forgive you.

Suddenly she stands up and waves.

Chris!

CHRIS *enters.*

She is poised, she is confident, she is well-dressed.

CHRIS. It seems a shame to waste the last day. Henry got his driver to drop me.

JOHN. Is he waiting?

CHRIS. No, we saw your car.

LIBBY *throws up the rug again so it is fully in the shade.*

CHRIS. His shadow will only move.

LIBBY. We can move with it!

She looks at the statue.

Much less erotic than the Greeks.

CHRIS. You haven't seen the boy in the museum in Alexandria.

She lies down on the rug.

She is in the shade but it will move off her.

At least I don't have to warn you about the perils of sunstroke when you're giving a lecture tomorrow.

LIBBY. At least you don't.

CHRIS. You'd be surprised how often it does happen. Instead of the bright lights of a lecture hall people end up in darkened rooms covered in calamine lotion.

JOHN. It's more a British Council problem than ours.

CHRIS. HM's government. Likes to get it's money's worth by keeping people as busy as possible.

LIBBY. I know!

CHRIS. Has he been dragging you round every single thing?

LIBBY. I've been a bit disappointing really, haven't I?

JOHN. Not everybody's as interested. Have you packed?

CHRIS. More or less. Thank God the climate in Tunis is the same.

LIBBY. Makes travelling much easier.

CHRIS. You always store your cold country clothes, but I don't know when you look at them again –

She looks at JOHN *who is hovering.*

You have to brief me on the Min. of Ag's visit.

JOHN *nods.*

I'm going to find out all sorts of things that I knew were going on but I didn't know about. Henry says it won't take more than 20 minutes.

JOHN. We'll have time at the airport.

CHRIS. Yes. Your hotel's all fixed. Do you mind being moved when John gets back?

LIBBY. I can't do anything until I get back from the university anyway.

CHRIS. Even if you weren't you don't get hotel rooms here 'til after midday.

JOHN. If you'd both excuse me, there's a set of reliefs of flax gathering I'd like to look at.

CHRIS. Flax is one of the crops we should suggest.

LIBBY. They'd get more for it than they get for their potatoes!

But JOHN *doesn't go.*

CHRIS. You might as well as while you're here.

LIBBY. If we get abducted by a camel driver we'll scream.

JOHN. Any sheik who abducted you here would charge you for the camel ride!

He goes.

CHRIS *watches him go.*

LIBBY. Are you looking forward to it?

CHRIS. Now the sorting out's done, yes. John will keep an eye on you, everyone will see you don't get bored or lonely.

LIBBY. And who does that to you?

CHRIS. I will have a mountain of work. And years of experience. I take a favourite book and a table-cloth. At least that's what I always used to do. I must remember about the table-cloth.

She gets out a notebook and writes it down.

LIBBY. The list.

CHRIS. Oh yes, the list.

LIBBY. I bought you a present.

She hands CHRISTINE *a rag doll made of scraps.*

CHRIS. Thank you.

LIBBY. And this one for me. We can swap if you prefer.

CHRIS. How much?

LIBBY. Five pounds.

CHRIS. Each?

LIBBY. It's all hand sewn.

CHRIS. The going rate's one. She tell you she needed it for school?

LIBBY. Yes.

CHRIS. You've been had.

LIBBY. I know. I saw her. She went straight off and spent it on Coca Cola. She turned round and grinned at me.

CHRIS. It upsets some visitors dreadfully. That's it, no one can touch them for anything again.

LIBBY. She could have at least waited until I was out of sight.

CHRIS. Why?

LIBBY. I suppose I knew. I just didn't want to see.

CHRIS. You want her to spend her money in the way you think she should.

LIBBY. It's her long-term future I'm concerned with. It doesn't matter. I can afford it. Next time I'll bargain.

She fiddles with the doll.

They reminded me of our lives. All the bits.

CHRIS. Yes!

LIBBY. I think I'd prefer to forget this bit of me.

CHRIS. You'd fall apart.

LIBBY. I could –

She distorts the doll.

I couldn't.

CHRIS. Not without becoming a very odd shape.

LIBBY. My head's fallen off.

CHRIS. You were warned.

LIBBY *unravels the stuffing from the head.*

Something that is visible.

Lurid green wool or something.

CHRIS. If Henry only knew!

LIBBY. Some days I wish it was.

CHRIS. Make for an easier life.

LIBBY. Is that why you married John?

CHRIS. He married me to stop me going to Brazil. I was a flier.

Went in after him and ended up further up the ladder. And a woman and not quite –. He didn't take orders from me the way he does from Henry. If it was a case of discussion he'd end up saying 'I agree but – .' The job in Brazil was a very good one. He was certainly jealous I'd been offered it.

LIBBY. Do you believe that?

CHRIS. On a bad day.

LIBBY. On a good day?

CHRIS. He didn't want me to go to Brazil because he loved me.

LIBBY. There you are.

CHRIS. But if he loved me, why couldn't he have come to Brazil? If he loved me he'd make me stay now. All I want is to be happy, it's not much to ask is it?

LIBBY. Not much.

CHRIS. What happened?

LIBBY. When?

CHRIS. Between the two of you. At Bristol?

LIBBY. We were lovers.

CHRIS. Oh.

LIBBY. Yes.

CHRIS. I don't know why I needed to know.

LIBBY. It's over.

CHRIS. Is it?

LIBBY. I hope so.

JOHN *comes back in.*

CHRIS. Interesting?

JOHN. Other people must have suggested flax to them. Libby, you really ought to see the Step Pyramid.

LIBBY. I can't bear it.

Pause.

LIBBY. Too much death. None of it is about looking forward

and planning. None of it is about being happy.

She has got up and walked away from them.

Is it better? Is any of it better?

JOHN. People have made vast strides.

LIBBY. Do you really think that?

JOHN. Yes I do.

CHRIS. Do you believe it?

JOHN. Of course I believe it if I think it.

CHRIS. Oh!

JOHN. What do you mean, oh?

CHRIS. Just, oh!

JOHN. Oh?

CHRIS. You aren't at work. You don't have to wring it for every meaning.

JOHN (*to* LIBBY). What do you think the past 3,000 years has been about if it hasn't been progress?

LIBBY. I don't know.

JOHN. Well we're not dead.

CHRIS. That's a great consolation!

JOHN. Any time but the last hundred years, statistically we would have been by now.

LIBBY. It also depends on who we are and where we are.

JOHN. Well of course.

LIBBY. So where is the progress?

JOHN. It can't all happen overnight.

LIBBY. It isn't happening.

JOHN. Look at what you're involved in.

LIBBY. In 50 years there'll still be people starving!

JOHN. But less of them.

CHRIS. I don't want anybody starving.

JOHN. None of us do.

CHRIS *is lying and watching the sun move off her arm.*

LIBBY. Then why don't we cancel the third world debt?

JOHN. Because you know it's not so easy. People have to pay for what they've got.

LIBBY. What about what we've got?

JOHN. Do you really think if we sent back the Sphinx's beard they would look after it?

CHRIS. It would be a great way of selling glue.

LIBBY. But it's not what I mean.

JOHN. So Libby what are you ready to give up?

LIBBY. I'm ready to give up the guilt.

CHRIS. Libby, you of all people have least cause to be guilty.

JOHN. I'm expecting a telex from Nairobi.

LIBBY. What are you expecting it to say?

JOHN. I wasn't responsible for your reception there.

LIBBY. No, I was.

JOHN. That's why we want to get everything clear.

LIBBY. I'm the only person responsible for it.

JOHN. You were there at their invitation. Whatever you had to say they should have listened.

LIBBY. Because what could I promise them? I'm here to encourage you to have two children. Why? Isn't that the question you'd ask?

JOHN. I'd have thought the answers were obvious.

LIBBY. Of course they are to us.

CHRIS. It's why we send people like you.

LIBBY. To say what! The obvious things! The reason that people in your country are starving is because you're reproducing yourselves too much!

JOHN. Africa's got to feed herself.

LIBBY. Africa could feed herself. But we don't let her, do we?

JOHN. We give all the help we can.

CHRIS. We don't.

Pause.

We want our coffee and our ground nut oil.

LIBBY. We want what we can get. How can I tell them to feed themselves when I come from a country that can't feed itself?

JOHN. We could feed ourselves.

LIBBY. But we don't. We buy, of course we buy cheaply, we all like a bargain.

JOHN. Without their exports –

CHRIS. What?

JOHN. What would happen to their balance of payments?

CHRIS. Do we need to ship in new potatoes for the QBP?

JOHN. The QBP celebrates our – well our – they appreciate knowing what people in England eat.

LIBBY. And the Scots and the Welsh.

CHRIS. The Irish?

JOHN. Okay, it's symbolic but it does sum up a concept.

LIBBY. Of what?

JOHN. What we are.

CHRIS. My mother buys Egyptian potatoes because they're cheaper.

JOHN. The flavour –

LIBBY. The flavour –

CHRIS. She can't afford the flavour. She has no choice. A potato is a potato and the cheaper it comes the better.

LIBBY. So what was I supposed to tell them? All the things I knew. What about all the other things I know. That the people we most want to reach are the people who have least vested interest?

JOHN. Everybody has a vested interest.

CHRIS. Unless they are poor.

JOHN. If they go on having huge families it's their own fault.

CHRIS. Oh it's always our fault!

JOHN. People have to make an effort.

LIBBY. They have to know what for.

JOHN. The rewards are obvious. A better standard of living for all.

LIBBY. Whose standard of living improves?

JOHN. Everyone's.

CHRIS. Not the people's at the bottom of the heap. They stay at the bottom. Granted the bottom might be a damn sight nicer with a washing machine but it is still the bottom even in clean clothes.

JOHN. If those people then have five children –

CHRIS. My parents only had me.

JOHN. And look at what you've done for them?

LIBBY. If there'd been five of her they might have got five times as much. That's the logic. That's why those are the people it's hardest to reach.

CHRIS. When I took Kit home with me last summer, all he wanted to know was why people didn't get away. Why they didn't leave it all behind and go somewhere there were jobs and there was money. He'd never been in a council house –

JOHN. It's not a council house, you bought it for her.

CHRIS. Yes, I did, because she wanted me to and I didn't think it was very much to ask. She is my mother, Libby.

LIBBY. I can understand that.

CHRIS. He was expecting the streets to be full of people in rags. That's the poverty he's seen. The poverty he knows how to see. Why have those people got a car? Why don't they sell their car and buy a house somewhere nicer? But they can't sell the car because there are no buses. They don't have a choice. So they live with not choosing and they live in fear of the people who can choose. Because they think a choice that's made must be right. So the people who make it must be right.

LIBBY. So why should they have listened to me? Would you listen to a stranger who cannot put her hand on her heart and tell you how the problem should be solved? Would you listen when that stranger comes from a country that urges you to change your ways but won't help you by changing its own? Would you want to hear that that is the real truth of the matter when it's a truth you know anyway? Why should you listen? I wouldn't have done. And not because I never listen, because that isn't true, but because why should I be that polite. I didn't have an answer. And an answer is what is wanted.

She stops.

She is exhausted.

JOHN. What is the answer?

LIBBY. Aren't you the people that are supposed to tell me?

JOHN. Why am I supposed to know?

LIBBY. Because you sit there holding authority.

JOHN. I can assure you if an apology is in order –

CHRIS. We should be apologising.

JOHN. Why?

CHRIS. Because it is our fault.

JOHN. Chris, whatever went wrong in the past, it's not us that are to blame.

LIBBY. We have to admit the fault or we go on being guilty.

JOHN. We are doing everything we can.

CHRIS. We won't even impose sanctions on South Africa!

LIBBY. The chairwoman kept patting my hand. And saying we'd just wait for silence. That would have been worse because then I would have had to say. I didn't want them to have to listen to me because I knew the things that I was going to say were the only things I could say – And I try and I try and I try to understand but I can only understand through my understanding which is white and well-educated and which expects things and therefore hopes and therefore despairs.

CHRIS. Don't despair.

LIBBY. I can't do anything. It's people like you who could do things and you don't.

Pause.

Would you mind if I went back?

CHRIS *sits up.*

JOHN (*looking at his watch*). It's about time.

LIBBY. I'd prefer to get a taxi if there's someone there to let me in.

CHRIS. Yusef's there.

She goes.

CHRIS *and* JOHN *are left alone together.*

JOHN. I wouldn't want her to get lost.

CHRIS. Let her go.

She gets out her notebook.

The Minister of Agriculture?

JOHN. Fact-finding.

CHRIS. What does he want to find?

JOHN. That the exchange of information programme works.

CHRIS. Does it.?

JOHN. For them. They don't have any information we need, so I'd say it doesn't.

CHRIS. The Egyptians need it.

JOHN. There are other places they could get the help and HM's government wouldn't be paying.

CHRIS. So we don't give any more?

JOHN. We haven't got it to give, not unless we're getting it back in some way.

CHRIS. With interest?

JOHN. That's what it's about. I'll give you all the relevant papers.

CHRIS. I think Henry's giving me the brief so I have an excuse for 'phone calls.

JOHN. I'll look forward to it.

CHRIS. What are you going to do about Kit?

JOHN. When?

CHRIS. I don't think it's something you should do over the 'phone.

JOHN. What if he wants to speak to you?

CHRIS. He can have my number.

JOHN. And what will you say?

CHRIS. Why would you never make me his guardian?

JOHN. You know why.

CHRIS. Because I don't quite belong?

JOHN. Because I thought Vee was best.

CHRIS. More reliable?

JOHN. At the moment it looks like it. Things will be fine with Vee once he's apologised.

CHRIS. Isn't an apology a bit strong?

JOHN. No.

CHRIS. It just seems a bit hypocritical.

JOHN. I don't think she was asking him to go down on bended knee.

CHRIS. But if he doesn't believe –

JOHN. That's not an excuse for him upsetting people who do.

CHRIS. It's dishonest!

JOHN. Isn't going to Tunis?

CHRIS. What do you mean?

JOHN. You're too clever to sell your soul.

CHRIS. I'm not selling my soul.

JOHN. Yes you are.

CHRIS. Because I want to belong? Is there anything wrong in belonging. I thought it was disgusting the first time I saw people eating asparagus. Using their fingers. The people I'd been brought up to emulate. The people I thought knew better.

JOHN. That's how it's eaten.

CHRIS. I know that now. But I didn't and that's what makes the knowledge special. I want to belong.

JOHN. You do belong.

CHRIS. WHERE!

Tell me where!

WHERE!

WHERE!

To all the things I gave up for my career? If I belong back in Hexham haven't I let them all down? All the sacrifices they made so I could go beyond them. The times they never stood in my way. Never said that it hurt. Never said 'Please don't go' but always said 'Go'. Even my father when he was dying, pretending he was fine so I'd take Switzerland because it was First Secretary. Even though he hadn't a clue what a First Secretary was and thought that that was where you started. Not where most people considered they'd done well to have finished. And me pretending that he would get better and that I'd take them to see the Swiss lakes because that was what he wanted for me.

To the diplomatic services because – because it is where I wanted to be.

To you? When I can't. Because I'm frightened to. Because you might let me down. And there was so long without you. And I thought you or whoever you were would never happen.

Because I want to stay?

JOHN. I love you, Christine.

CHRIS. Because I want to believe in love?

JOHN. Then believe.

CHRIS. I'm too frightened.

I know how to deal with struggling into a cocktail frock in the ladies lavatory. I know how to pacify an irate cabinet minister. I can do those things.

In order to survive, I have to think better than I feel. And when I stop thinking, what is there left?

Is there anything?

JOHN *reaches out to touch her.*

I can't feel it!

He holds her tighter.

I can't.

Pause.

It has to be a choice doesn't it?

JOHN. Yes.

CHRIS. And I have to choose.

She becomes matter of fact.

I'll explain to Yusef about the asparagus. And new potatoes have to go in boiling water. With mint.

And we'll stop on the way to the airport and get you another pair of black shoes, so you'll always have a clean pair.

JOHN *takes off his shoes and throws them as far into the desert as he can.*

It is a shocking moment.

And then CHRIS *begins to laugh.*

It's not hysterical laughter.

Then CHRIS *starts to move in the direction of the shoes.*

JOHN. Where are you going?

CHRIS. To get your shoes.

JOHN. Leave them.

CHRIS. Somebody will take them.

JOHN. So?

CHRIS. You won't have any shoes.

JOHN. I won't have to go to the QBP.

CHRIS. If I stay now, they'll never give me another chance.

JOHN. I understand that. Shall I come with you?

CHRIS. No. I have to be the one that chooses.

She moves towards him.

JOHN. What I had meant was Tunis.

They kiss. (If it seems appropriate).

JOHN. Bloody hell Christine, they're stealing them!

They rush out, scaring children.

Scene Three

JOHN *and* CHRIS's *garden. There is a swimming pool. There are outdoor tables and chairs. It is after the QBP. Not that there is debris everywhere but the garden has taken quite a pounding.*

JOHN *enters. He has some sort of receptacle for rubbish with him. He picks up the last few bits of rubbish.*

CHRIS *comes out. She is wearing a wrap of some sort over her swimming costume. Her feet are bare. A swim is going to be her response to the day.*

JOHN *looks at her.*

JOHN. We're 11 glasses down.

CHRIS. Oh.

She disappears for a moment and comes back with sandels that she puts on.

I can account for seven.

And –

She finds a wine glass which is full of wine.

JOHN. If the Muslim's want orange juice why don't they ask for orange juice?

CHRIS. Because they don't want to offend us.

She chucks the wine into a bush.

JOHN. I find that more offensive.

CHRIS. I think it was probably one of the French. Don't you think English wine is taking things a bit too far?

JOHN. I thought the white was all right.

CHRIS. That's still three

She hunts round the garden for the missing wine glasses.

JOHN. Kit used to love it. He thought it was a great game.

CHRIS (*looking into the swimming pool*). I just hope they aren't at the bottom of here.

JOHN. I doubt they'll be broken. The water resistance.

CHRIS *is walking along the edge of the swimming pool.*

Did you know about my Sony Walkman?

CHRIS. Did I now what about it?

JOHN. Did you know that's what Kit had bought me for my birthday?

CHRIS. John, it's a secret.

JOHN. It's not a secret now I know about it.

CHRIS. What do you want to know about it?

JOHN. Why did he think I wanted a Sony Walkman?

CHRIS. To listen to on the plane.

She's accumulated some rubbish.

She comes to the rubbish container to dispose of it.

JOHN. Why?

CHRIS. Why? Because it's what he does on planes. What he likes doing on planes.

JOHN. It must have been terribly expensive.

CHRIS. It was 19.99 at the Heathrow duty free.

JOHN. You mean he bought it there, brought it here and then took it all the way back again?

CHRIS. You're going to be in England for your birthday. This is the boy you think lives only in the moment.

JOHN. I'm not getting it now he's giving it to Vee as a peace offering. I suppose I could send him the money for it.

CHRIS. Then he'd know I told you how much it cost.

She takes a chair and climbs up to rescue a glass that has been put somewhere up on a ledge.

We know who put that there. Erica says he does exactly the same at the American Embassy. And that he lives in fear of someone being posted here who is taller. So he puts wine glasses on the highest place he can find as his calling card. Two. That's a record.

JOHN. One'll be in Henry's pocket and he'll bring it back tomorrow.

CHRIS. That's only one then.

JOHN. The grass will never recover.

CHRIS. You say that every year, wherever we are. You'll be saying it in Washington.

JOHN. Or Paris –

Pause.

CHRIS. Or Moscow. I'll count against you.

JOHN. It doesn't matter.

CHRIS. They'll have me down as unreliable.

JOHN. The only person you have to be reliable to is you.

CHRIS. And you. Staying ought to count in our favour.

JOHN. We just have to show them that it does.

I think they probably hug here.

CHRIS. I didn't stay to ruin things for you.

JOHN. The only thing ruined is the grass. Chrissie, I won't get the big jobs anyway.

CHRIS. Moscow might be a problem since you don't speak Russian.

JOHN. I'm being honest. Don't play.

CHRIS. I thought that's what you wanted.

JOHN. It was. And I wanted if for you too.

CHRIS. I never wanted it. I wanted you to have what you wanted. Indulging them in a dream's not much to give someone.

JOHN. You could have thrown it back at me.

CHRIS. It would have hurt too much.

JOHN. When did you realise?

CHRIS. I've always realised.

JOHN. Even when we got married?

CHRIS. Yes.

JOHN. Then why did you pretend?

CHRIS. Because the first time I met you at university and asked you what you were going to do when you left, you said British Ambassador in Washington.

JOHN. I meant it.

CHRIS. I know you did.

JOHN. I didn't mean to let you down.

CHRIS. You haven't let me down.

JOHN. I'm sorry, Christine.

CHRIS. I wanted to marry you. Not what you had been not what you're going to become. You.

JOHN. I'm sorry.

CHRIS. At least this way we get to see each other. I get desperate now for us to sit down and have a boiled egg together.

JOHN. I will try, Christine. You do come first.

CHRIS. I have to know it.

JOHN. What is it?

CHRIS. Time.

JOHN. I don't have to stay in the service.

CHRIS. You'd hate leaving.

JOHN. We could find something we could do together.

CHRIS. We're doing this together.

JOHN. You hate the QBP!

CHRIS. Everybody hates the QBP.

    JOHN *finds a plate of uneaten food.*

JOHN. Even the guests.

    CHRIS *dips her finger into the mess.*

    It is something with strawberries.

CHRIS. It's hollandaise sauce.

    JOHN *trashes it.*

    However simple it is, it's not always going to be understood.

JOHN. I'd like to be home when Kit does his 'A' levels.

CHRIS. He could have a pet.

JOHN. You are not to encourage him to be a farmer!

CHRIS. There's nothing wrong with farming.

JOHN. The boy's never been anywhere near a farm!

CHRIS. Yes, but he knows farmers are tied hand and foot and don't have holidays and aren't made to go abroad. Libby says if we really want him put off we can send him to help George in February.

JOHN. What do you think?

CHRIS. Why not?

JOHN. It was never like this with Libby, Chris.

CHRIS. Good.

JOHN. Why isn't Yusef doing this?

CHRIS. It was our party.

Enter LIBBY.

LIBBY. I was expecting it to look like a bomb site. I found this by the gate.

She holds out a wine glass.

JOHN. We've done it! We've actually done it!

CHRIS. We can account for every glass.

JOHN *whirls* CHRIS *round in delight.*

LIBBY. Erica sends her apologies.

CHRIS. I told you it becomes impossible to find the time to fit people in. Are you okay?

LIBBY. A bit homesick, that's all.

CHRIS. Not long now.

LIBBY. No.

JOHN. Is George picking you up?

LIBBY. He always does. Not in the winter. I pay a taxi driver to take the risks.

CHRIS. I envy you the winter.

LIBBY. Not the snow and the ice and the rain.

CHRIS. Not the snow and the ice and the rain but our idea of it.

LIBBY. Think of me envying you this. Whatever I think about it I can't not. I would like a house with servants and a swimming pool.

JOHN. We'd like to take you up on your offer to have Kit.

LIBBY *pauses.*

LIBBY. Thanks. A last swim.

CHRIS. Don't you go in the sea?

LIBBY. At Temadoc. You must be joking.

She goes in to get changed.

CHRIS *contemplates the wine glass.*

CHRIS. I can't bear it if Henry doesn't have one in his pocket.

JOHN. We could ring and ask.

CHRIS. I don't think Henry would appreciate that coming from me.

JOHN. He brought this for Libby.

CHRIS. What is it?

JOHN. The apology from Nairobi.

CHRIS. Oh.

JOHN. They sent it.

CHRIS. Did we ask them?

JOHN. Not from this end.

CHRIS. Kenya?

JOHN. No, I think it was the organisers off their own bat.

CHRIS. She gave me a copy to read.

JOHN. I'd like to see it.

CHRIS. She asked me not to.

JOHN. Should I give this to her?

CHRIS. She's going to think we asked.

JOHN. That's Libby.

CHRIS. Do we have to give it her?

JOHN. It's a small world. If we don't and someone says it's been sent –

CHRIS. The problem with the QBP is that is causes absolute choas. Nothing gets properly sorted out for weeks.

JOHN. All right.

He throws the telex into the garbage bag.

CHRIS. Thank you. Are you going to come in?

JOHN. What does your conscience do about the swimming pool?

CHRIS. It's not mine. It's Her Majesty's. I'm just borrowing.

She starts putting on her swimming hat.

Be a mirror. Okay?

JOHN. You're going to have one little wet bit.

He pulls her to him and pushes a bit of hair up into her swimming cap.

It becomes an embrace.

They stand.

The sunset is pink.

CHRIS. There's one advantage to Britain. In the summer the days take longer to die. Hurry up or it will be too dark.

But still he stands.

LIBBY *comes out in her swimming costume.*

She stands with them for a moment.

LIBBY. I wish my flight was now, this moment, so I could just be home.

JOHN. Would you like a drink?

CHRIS (*pushing him – it's playful*). She'd like you to stop being diplomatic and get changed.

JOHN. I'm going!

He goes in.

CHRIS. Quick, before John gets in. He does very serious lengths and never looks where he's going. If you collide not only do you get drowned but also blamed.

LIBBY *takes off her wrap and climbs into the pool.*

CHRIS *stands on the side and watches.*

This time tomorrow you'll be home.

The rest of the conversation takes places while LIBBY *swims.*

LIBBY. Where's home for you?

CHRIS. Here.

The light is going fast now.

John is home. No walls, no roof, no floor. The flood could sweep through any time.

JOHN *shouts out of the house.*

JOHN. Where are my trunks?

CHRIS. Look on the line.
Did your mother promise you that when you were grown up, you would be able to do whatever you wanted?

LIBBY. Yes.

CHRIS. Do you think you are doing what you wanted?

LIBBY. Some days. Do you?

CHRIS. Some days.

CHRIS *takes off her wrap and climbs into the pool.*

There is a splash as CHRIS *goes under the water.*

There is silence except for the sound of them swimming as the light fades.

Darkness.

The sound of swimming.